# 10th Meeting of the ACL Special Interest Group on Computational Morphology and Phonology 2008

# (SIGMORPHON 2008)



**Held in conjunction with ACL-HLT 2008**

## Columbus, Ohio, USA
## 19 June 2008

**ISBN: 978-1-61738-549-0**

**Printed from e-media with permission by:**

Curran Associates, Inc.
57 Morehouse Lane
Red Hook, NY 12571
www.proceedings.com

**Some format issues inherent in the e-media version may also appear in this print version.**



Printed by Curran Associates, Inc. (2010)



Association for Computational Linguistics
209 N. Eighth Street
Stroudsburg, Pennsylvania 18360

Phone: 1-570-476-8006
Fax: 1-570-476-0860

acl@aclweb.org

# Introduction

We are pleased to present the Proceedings of the Tenth Meeting of the ACL Special Interest Group on Computational Morphology and Phonology (SIGMORPHON), to be held on June 19, 2008 at Ohio State University in Columbus, Ohio.

The purpose of SIGMORPHON is to foster computational research on the phonological, morphological, and phonetic properties of human language. All three of these sub-areas deal largely with the local structure of words and so share many technical methods. Furthermore, computational work that models empirical data must often draw on at least two of these areas, with explicit consideration of the morphology-phonology or phonology-phonetics interface.

Morphology and phonetics were officially added to the SIG's charter only in 2006, when the SIG membership voted to amend the SIG's constitution and change its name from SIGPHON. This expansion of the SIG's mission beyond phonology was supported and subsequently approved by the ACL. The new name (suggested by Johanna Moore) is pronounced "SIG *more* fun," which we hope is an accurate assessment.

Since SIGMORPHON's 2007 workshop was a special-topic workshop on computing and historical phonology, the present 2008 workshop is the first that reflects the breadth of the new charter. In particular, we are pleased to include two papers on unsupervised morphological analysis, and an invited talk on articulatory modeling for speech recognition.

We are grateful to the program committee for their careful and thoughtful reviews and discussions of the papers submitted this year. Just over half of the submissions were accepted on first review, with an additional submission accepted after revisions. We also thank this year's invited speakers, Karen Livescu and Jason Riggle, for presenting their noteworthy work to the SIGMORPHON community.

We hope that you enjoy the workshop and these proceedings.

Jason Eisner
Jeffrey Heinz

**Organizers:**

Jason Eisner, Johns Hopkins University
Jeffrey Heinz, University of Delaware

**Program Committee Members:**

Adam Albright, Massachusetts Institute of Technology
Lynne Cahill, University of Brighton
Mathias Creutz, Helsinki University of Technology
Mark Ellison, University of Western Australia
Eric Fosler-Lussier, Ohio State University
John Goldsmith, University of Chicago
Sharon Goldwater, Stanford University
Katrin Kirchhoff, University of Washington
Greg Kondrak, University of Alberta
Ying Lin, University of Arizona
Mike Maxwell, University of Maryland
John Nerbonne, University of Groningen
Kemal Oflazer, Sabanci University
Jason Riggle, University of Chicago
Richard Sproat, University of Illinois
Richard Wicentowski, Swarthmore University
Shuly Wintner, University of Haifa

**Invited Speakers:**

Karen Livescu, Toyota Technological Institute at Chicago
Jason Riggle, University of Chicago

# Table of Contents


*Invited talk: Phonological Models in Automatic Speech Recognition*
Karen Livescu . . . . . 1

*Bayesian Learning over Conflicting Data: Predictions for Language Change*
Rebecca Morley . . . . . 2

*A Bayesian Model of Natural Language Phonology: Generating Alternations from Underlying Forms*
David Ellis . . . . . 12

*Unsupervised Word Segmentation for Sesotho Using Adaptor Grammars*
Mark Johnson . . . . . 20

*Invited talk: Counting Rankings*
Jason Riggle . . . . . 28

*Three Correlates of the Typological Frequency of Quantity-Insensitive Stress Systems*
Max Bane and Jason Riggle . . . . . 29

*Phonotactic Probability and the Maori Passive: A Computational Approach*
'Ōiwi Parker Jones . . . . . 39

*Evaluating an Agglutinative Segmentation Model for ParaMor*
Christian Monson, Alon Lavie, Jaime Carbonell and Lori Levin . . . . . 49

# Workshop Program

**Thursday, June 19, 2008**

| | |
|---|---|
| 8:50–9:00 | Opening remarks |
| 9:00–10:00 | *Invited talk: Phonological Models in Automatic Speech Recognition*<br>Karen Livescu |
| 10:00–10:30 | *Bayesian Learning over Conflicting Data: Predictions for Language Change*<br>Rebecca Morley |
| 10:30–11:00 | Break |
| 11:00–11:30 | *A Bayesian Model of Natural Language Phonology: Generating Alternations from Underlying Forms*<br>David Ellis |
| 11:30–12:00 | *Unsupervised Word Segmentation for Sesotho Using Adaptor Grammars*<br>Mark Johnson |
| 12:00–14:00 | Lunch |
| 14:00–15:00 | *Invited talk: Counting Rankings*<br>Jason Riggle |
| 15:00–15:30 | *Three Correlates of the Typological Frequency of Quantity-Insensitive Stress Systems*<br>Max Bane and Jason Riggle |
| 15:30–16:00 | Break |
| 16:00–16:30 | *Phonotactic Probability and the Maori Passive: A Computational Approach*<br>ʻŌiwi Parker Jones |
| 16:30–17:00 | *Evaluating an Agglutinative Segmentation Model for ParaMor*<br>Christian Monson, Alon Lavie, Jaime Carbonell and Lori Levin |
| 17:00–17:30 | General discussion |

# Invited Talk:
# Phonological Models in Automatic Speech Recognition

**Karen Livescu**
Toyota Technological Institute at Chicago
1427 E. 60th St., Chicago, IL 60637
klivescu@tti-c.org

## Abstract

The performance of automatic speech recognition systems varies widely across different contexts. Very good performance can be achieved on single-speaker, large-vocabulary dictation in a clean acoustic environment, as well as on very small vocabulary tasks with much fewer constraints on the speakers and acoustic conditions. In other domains, speech recognition is still far from usable for real-world applications. One domain that is still elusive is that of spontaneous conversational speech. This type of speech poses a number of challenges, such as the presence of disfluencies, a mix of speech and non-speech sounds such as laughter, and extreme variation in pronunciation. In this talk, I will focus on the challenge of pronunciation variation. A number of analyses suggest that this variability is responsible for a large part of the drop in recognition performance between read (dictated) speech and conversational speech.

I will describe efforts in the speech recognition community to characterize and model pronunciation variation, both for conversational speech and in general. The work can be roughly divided into several types of approaches, including: augmentation of a phonetic pronunciation lexicon with phonological rules; the use of large (syllable- or word-sized) units instead of the more traditional phonetic ones; and the use of *smaller* units, such as distinctive or articulatory features. Of these, the first is the most thoroughly studied and also the most disappointing: Despite successes in a few domains, it has been difficult to obtain significant recognition improvements by including in the lexicon those phonetic pronunciations that appear to exist in the data. In part as a reaction to this, many have advocated the use of a "null pronunciation model," i.e. a very limited lexicon including only canonical pronunciations. The assumption in this approach is that the observation model—the distribution of the acoustics given phonetic units—will better model the "noise" introduced by pronunciation variability.

I will advocate an alternative view: that the phone unit may not be the most appropriate for modeling the lexicon. When considering a variety of pronunciation phenomena, it becomes apparent that phonetic transcription often obscures some of the fundamental processes that are at play. I will describe approaches using both larger and "smaller" units. Larger units are typically syllables or words, and allow greater freedom to model the component states of each unit. In the class of "smaller" unit models, ideas from articulatory and autosegmental phonology motivate multi-tier models in which different features (or groups of features) have semi-independent behavior. I will present a particular model in which articulatory features are represented as variables in a dynamic Bayesian network.

Non-phonetic pronunciation models can involve significantly different model structures than those typically used in speech recognition, and as a result they may also entail modifications to other components such as the observation model and training algorithms. At this point it is not clear what the "winning" approach will be. The success of a given approach may depend on the domain or on the amount and type of training data available. I will describe some of the current challenges and ongoing work, with a particular focus on the role of phonological theories in statistical models of pronunciation (and vice versa?).



*Proceedings of the Tenth Meeting of the ACL Special Interest Group on Computational Morphology and Phonology*, page 1,
Columbus, Ohio, USA June 2008. 

# Bayesian Learning Over Conflicting Data: Predictions for language change

**Rebecca Morley**
Cognitive Science Department
Johns Hopkins University
3400 N. Charles St.
Baltimore, MD 21218
morley@cogsci.jhu.edu

## Abstract

This paper is an analysis of the claim that a universal ban on certain ('anti-markedness') grammars is necessary in order to explain their non-occurrence in the languages of the world. To assess the validity of this hypothesis I examine the implications of one sound change (a > ə) for learning in a specific phonological domain (stress assignment), making explicit assumptions about the type of data that results, and the learning function that computes over that data. The preliminary conclusion is that restrictions on possible end-point languages are unneeded, and that the most likely outcome of change is a lexicon that is inconsistent with respect to a single generating rule.

## 1 Introduction

The basic tenet of Evolutionary Phonology is that the observed universal commonalities in phonological systems of the world arise from the universal commonality of the way listeners and speakers produce and perceive sound structures (Blevins, 2004). Diachronic processes operating via the transmission of the speech signal act without regard for the subsequent system they create. Alternate theories in the tradition of Chomsky argue for universal prohibitions which would serve to ban or repair certain changes just in case they would result in a 'disallowed' system (Kiparsky 2004, 2006). In Optimality Theoretic terms, this would be a grammar that violates the canonical set of universal markedness constraints. I will call this claim the Universal-Grammar-Delimited Hypothesis Space (UG-Delimited $\mathcal{H}$) Principle.

Without this check, Kiparsky argues, common and natural sound changes ('blind' Evolutionary Phonology) would frequently produce unnatural and in fact unobserved 'anti-markedness' languages (such as a system in which lower sonority vowels were stressed in preference to higher sonority vowels).

An analysis of the properties of possible grammars is an analysis that involves explicitly characterizing the properties of the learner, as well as of the data to which the learner is exposed. The work in this paper is, to my knowledge, the first attempt to do exactly this kind of analysis, for exactly the type of scenario in which a dispreferred, but hypothetically learnable, grammar might arise.

Diachronic changes that are caused by factors outside of the grammar have the capability of disrupting a categorical rule system, introducing irregularities into a previously regular pattern. These irregularities may have an 'unnatural' or anti-markedness character, but typically, they will coexist alongside remnants of the prior natural pattern. That is the first observation. The second is that if learners are allowed to adopt mixed-grammar hypotheses ('co-phonologies' (Inkelas 1997), 'stratal faithfulness' (Ito and Mester 2001), 'lexical indexation' (Pater 2000)), then under a posterior-maximizing learning model, these hybrid systems are the most likely outcome (rather than a categorical 'anti-markedness' grammar).

I will work through a case study of sonority sensitive stress, paying special attention to the lexicon that would be produced after a hypothetical sound change of the type Kiparsky proposes. By examining the output of Bayesian hypothesis testing in this domain I will conclude that for the pure anti-markedness grammar to arise, not only is a



*Proceedings of the Tenth Meeting of the ACL Special Interest Group on Computational Morphology and Phonology*, pages 2–11, Columbus, Ohio, USA June 2008. ©2008 Association for Computational Linguistics

certain type of diachronic change necessary, but also a certain type of non-uniform lexical distribution. To first approximation, this confluence of circumstances appears rather rare, leading me to tentatively reject the hypothesis that categorical bans on allowed grammars are necessary to explain the distribution of the world's languages.

## 2 Gujarati Phonology

Kiparsky uses Gujarati to provide a concrete illustration of the relevant phonological paradigm: a sonority-sensitive stress system that respects the posited universal implicational hierarchy. There are eight vowels in Gujarati, corresponding to three sonority tiers: low: (ə), mid: (i,e,ɛ,o,ɔ,u), and high: (a). The stress system is described as conforming to the following position- and sonority- dependent rules.

<u>[1] *GUJARATI*: Sonority & Position -to-Stress</u>

- stress penultimate [a] (the most sonorous vowel)
- otherwise stress ante-penultimate [a]
- otherwise stress final [a]
- otherwise stress penultimate mid-sonority vowel (any of [i,e,ɛ,o,ɔ,u])
- otherwise stress ante-penultimate mid-sonority vowel
- otherwise stress the penultimate position (which must be [ə] (the lowest sonority vowel))

This type of system is easily describable within a standard OT framework (Prince and Smolensky 1993/2004) that utilizes a universally ordered sonority scale with respect to the markedness of (or dispreference for) stressing a particular vowel. Crucially, however, the reverse type of system, in which lower sonority vowels are the ones that attract stress, is so far unattested, and predicted, within the same framework, to be impossible.

### 2.1 Gujarati′

In stating his claim about the necessity of intrinsic bans on possible grammars, Kiparsky makes the following assumption: A common and natural type of sound change is one in which all a's of a language change to ə's [1]. I will adopt this assumption as well for the sake of argument, leaving aside a discussion of the evidence for how plausible it may be. It should be kept in mind that this particular change is being considered only as a stand-in for a class of possible sound changes that could produce similar outcomes with respect to markedness implications.

A change in vowel quality (with unchanged stress placement) will alter the make-up of the Gujarati lexicon, and raise the possibility of a system in which stress preferentially falls on the lowest-sonority vowel, [ə] (formerly [a], the most sonorous vowel)[2]. This new lexicon will, in turn, act as the input to the learner of Gujarati′. To determine the outcome of learning over this data set, some sort of characterization of the learner's hypothesis space is necessary. The list in [2] represents the full hypothesis set considered in this paper[3]. To begin, I will consider only hypotheses 1)-3), leaving aside the discussion of hypotheses 4) and 5) until Section 3.3.

<u>[2] $\mathcal{H}$:Hypothesis Space</u>

1) *PENULT*: Stress Penultimate Vowel
2) *GUJARATI*: Sonority & Position -to-Stress
3) *GUJARATI**: Reversed-Sonority & Position -to-Stress[4]
4) *NULL(G*/G)*: *GUJARATI** and *GUJARATI* equally likely generators of data
5) *MAX(G*/G)*: mixed-grammar of *GUJARATI** and *GUJARATI* with variable weights

[1] In fact, it is not clear how likely an internally motivated language change of a completely general nature is. What might be more plausible is that such changes would depend very heavily on context, with tokens that were less fully realized (e.g., shorter) being more likely to undergo the change than more fully /a/-like tokens. This, of course, would be correlated with their stress status.

[2] An alternative traditional generativist account, rather than admitting an anti-markedness hypothesis, might propose a difference between stress-attracting ə's and non-stress-attracting ə's based on differences in their underlying representations, effectively encoding the diachronic change within the synchronic grammar. This type of analytic bias will impede or prevent changes from affecting the rule system (grammar) of a language, and thus it is not pursued in the present work.

[3] This is clearly far from the only way in which the learning problem can be formulated. Given that this is, to my knowledge, the first study of its kind, a number of somewhat arbitrary representational decisions had to be made. For the purposes of this work the given $\mathcal{H}$-space is the result of what I view as a minimal departure from the standard formalisms both of linguistic theory and Bayesian learning.

[4] As in [1], but with the sonority classes reversed.

## 2.2 Evidence to the Learner: Gujarati Lexicon

The hypothetical lexicon of Gujarati′ ($L'$) depends on the inventory of the old Gujarati ($L$). For a given possible Gujarati, $L$ is mapped to $L'$ via the sound change a > ə. To construct the space of $L$ I start by making a list of all possible word types, where the type depends on features that are relevant to the hypotheses under consideration, namely the vowel identities. This listing also corresponds to a particular lexicon $L_{MU} \in L$; this is the word inventory under what I will call the Minimal Lexicon Uniformity assumption: that all types are represented in equal numbers, and each type occurs exactly once. For 3-syllable words and an 8 vowel inventory, there are $8^3$, or 512 distinct types. For 2-syllable words, there are $8^2$, or 64 types.

Table 1 lists the word types for 3-syllable words. 'Case' refers to the type (vowel make-up) of the word before the hypothetical sound change (where M indicates any of the mid-sonority vowel class {i,e,ɛ,o,ɔ,u}). We will restrict ourselves for the moment to considering only the first three hypotheses in the space: *PENULT*(*P*), *GUJARATI*(*G*), and *GUJARATI**(*G**)).

| | Case | Gujarati Example L > L′ | # types H |
|---|---|---|---|
| 1 | (ə,(ə,M),a)<br>(M,ə,a)<br>(a,ə,M)<br>(a,ə,(ə,a)) | [pərikʃá]>[pərikʃə́] | 21 |
| 2 | (M,M,a)<br>(a,M,(M,a,ə)) | [hoʃijáɾ]>[hoʃijə́ɾ] | 84<br>G* |
| 3 | (M,a,(ə,M,a)) | [mubáɾək]>[mubə́ɾək] | 48<br>G*,P |
| 4 | ((ə,M), M,ə)<br>(ə,M,M) | [tʃum:ótəɾ]>[tʃum:ótəɾ] | 78<br>G,P |
| 5 | (M,ə,M)<br>(M,ə,ə) | [kójəldi]>[kójəldi] | 42<br>G |
| 6 | (a,a,(a,M))<br>(ə,(a,ə),(a,ə,M))<br>(M,M,M) | [aw:ánã]>[əw:ə́nə̃] | 239<br>G,G*,P |

Table 1. Uniform Gujarati Lexicon: three-syllable words (words taken from de Lacy (2006))

Each row represents positive evidence for some subset of the three hypotheses under consideration; the hypotheses consistent with a given case are specified in the last column below the type counts. For example, in Row 3, the word [mubáɾək] in Gujarati, with stress determined by the markedness-abiding grammar described in [1] has become [mubə́ɾək] in Gujarati′. This form now exhibits stress on the lowest (rather than the highest) sonority vowel in the word. This pattern is consistent with the anti-markedness grammar *GUJARATI**. However, the stress placement in this word is also consistent with the simple positional grammar *PENULT*. If we indicate the number of types that support none of the hypotheses as $A$ (=arbitrary), and the number that support all hypotheses as $N$ (= neutral), then we can calculate the total type counts in support of each hypothesis ($A=21;\ G^*=371;\ G=359;\ N=239;\ P=365;\ T=512$). Note that $G^*$ exceeds $P$ by six word types.

## 3 The Bayesian Learner

The numbers in Table 1 represent the make-up of a possible lexicon of Gujarati′, namely, $L_{MU}'$. This will act as the initial input to our Bayesian learner (for simplicity, all calculations in this section will be performed only for 3-syllable words).

The Bayesian model has been extensively applied to learning scenarios in a number of cognitive domains (e.g., Chater et al., 2006; Kemp et al., 2007; Kording and Wolpert, 2006; Tenenbaum et al., 2007), and involves a fairly minimal and intuitive apparatus. Bayes theorem, which provides a formula for computing the posterior probability of a hypothesis given the data, and thus a method for evaluating competing grammars, is given in (1).

$$p(h \mid d) = \frac{p(d \mid h)p(h)}{p(d)} \tag{1}$$

For the problem at hand, the members of $d$ are stress assignments corresponding to each of the $n$ words of the lexicon. The conditional probability of a stress assignment $d_i$ under hypothesis $h$ is more properly written as $p(d_i|h,y_i)$, where stress assignment (as can be seen from Table 1) depends on the particular word type $y_i$. I will assume that the conditional probability of each surface stressed form is independent of any other. The probability of the set $d$ given $h$ and $y$ (where $h$ = *GUJARATI**, *PENULT*, or *GUJARATI*) can then be expanded as the product of the probability of each member of $d$

given $h$ and each member of $y$ (see Equation (2)).

### 3.1 'Non-Deterministic' Hypothesis Space

Applying Bayes Theorem to the first three hypotheses of [2] returns a value of $p(h|d)=0$ for each grammar. To avoid this collapse (due to the existence of contradictory data), let us assign a small probability of error ($2\alpha$) under each hypothesis. For a given 3-syllable word type, $y$, there are three stress possibilities: $C = \{1,2,3\}$, and the stress class assigned by a given hypothesis $H_i$ is written as a function of the input word type: $H_i(y) \in C$. For the Non-Deterministic version of the same hypothesis, written as $H_i^\alpha$, stress will be assigned to the consistent position ($c=H_i(y)$) with probability $1-2\alpha$, and to either of the two inconsistent positions with probability $\alpha$. See [3].

[3] $H_i^\alpha$ : Non-Deterministic Version of $H_i$

$$p(c \mid H_i^\alpha, y) = \begin{cases} 1-2\alpha & c = H_i(y) \\ \alpha & c \neq H_i(y) \end{cases}$$

We are assessing the consequences of learning with no markedness biases, so we will let the prior probability in Equation (1) be uniform over the hypothesis space. Since we are concerned with the winner in any two-hypothesis competition, we will work with the ratio of their posteriors. Here the hypotheses *GUJARATI**$^\alpha$, *GUJARATI*$^\alpha$ and *PENULT*$^\alpha$ are the Non-Deterministic counterparts of the previously introduced hypotheses of the same names, and the numerical values of $G^*$, $P$ and $T$ are extracted from Table 1, under $L_{MU}'$ (and given at the end of Section 2.1).

$$\frac{p(GUJARATI^{*\alpha} \mid d)}{p(PENULT^{\alpha} \mid d)} = \frac{\prod_i p(d_i \mid GUJARATI^{*\alpha}, y_i)}{\prod_i p(d_i \mid PENULT^{\alpha}, y_i)}$$

$$\frac{\prod_{[d_i \neq G^*(y_i)]} \alpha \prod_{[d_i = G^*(y_i)]} (1-2\alpha)}{\prod_{[d_i \neq P(y_i)]} \alpha \prod_{[d_i = P(y_i)]} (1-2\alpha)} = \frac{\alpha^{T-G^*}(1-2\alpha)^{G^*}}{\alpha^{T-P}(1-2\alpha)^{P}} \qquad (2)$$

As we can see from Equation (2), the relative probability advantage is highly dependent on the magnitude of $\alpha$. Since $\alpha$ is an error term, it should remain relatively small. Within this constraint, we could allow the learner to fit this parameter based on maximizing hypothesis likelihood. For the 3-syllable uniform lexicon, $\alpha_{ML}$ computed with respect to *GUJARATI** is approximately .14. Using this value in Equation (2) we find that *GUJARATI**$^\alpha$ wins out over both *GUJARATI*$^\alpha$ and *PENULT*$^\alpha$ by several orders of magnitude: $\frac{p(G^* \mid d)}{p(P \mid d)} \approx 1.85 \times 10^4$; $\frac{p(G^* \mid d)}{p(G \mid d)} \approx 3.4 \times 10^8$.

This initial result seems to provide strong support for The UG-Delimited $\mathcal{H}$ Principle: the *GUJARATI** grammar seems overwhelmingly likely to arise, and yet is unattested. However, it is instructive to consider the inherent sensitivity of the Bayesian learner to quite small differences between the linguistic hypotheses in question. A discrepancy between data coverage of a mere 6 words, as seen in the above case, can lead to a hypothesis advantage of four orders of magnitude. And, in fact, a discrepancy of even 1 word can give a posterior advantage on the order of a factor of 5 or greater (depending on the value of $\alpha$). This result is the consequence of the extreme probability distribution over only two types of data (consistent and inconsistent -- with values close to 1 in the first case, and close to 0 in the second). Since the probability of an independent collection of outcomes (a particular input lexicon) is computed via multiplication, each additional difference in data coverage compounds the single point case, such that the ratio grows exponentially.

If this behavior is indeed a problem for our linguistic domain (where different sub-regions of phonological regularity are often observed to coexist stably in natural language (Inkelas 1997)) then there are various means at our disposal to modify the learning model. In the following section I will consider an alternative weighted decision metric; in Section 3.3 I will expand the hypothesis space to include mixed-grammar competitors; and in Section 4 I will alter the parameters of the learning rule to provide a more stringent threshold for success in hypothesis competition.

### 3.2 Optimal Bayes Classifier

So far, we have been implicitly assuming a winner-take-all classification strategy whereby the hypothesis with the highest likelihood given the data is the one selected by the learner, and all others discarded. Let us now consider, instead, the Optimal Bayes Classifier which categorizes new instances of data by taking a weighted sum of the predictions of all hypotheses in the space.

As expressed in Equation (3), the probability that a new word $y$ will be assigned to category $c_m$ (stress syllable $m$), given the body of training data $d$ — $p(c_m|d,y)$ — is the weighted sum of the probability each hypothesis gives of $c_m$ classification — $p(c_m|H_s,y)$ — where each of these terms is weighted by the a posteriori probability of the particular hypothesis given the training data, $p(H_s \mid d)$.

$$p(c_m \mid d,y) = \sum_{H_s} p(c_m \mid H_s,y)\,p(H_s \mid d) \qquad (3)$$

Consider now the situation where there are three hypotheses in the space: $H_i^\alpha$, $H_j^\alpha$, and $H_k^\alpha$. The formulation of the selector function in Equation (3) allows for the possibility of a ganging-up effect whereby $H_j^\alpha$ and $H_k^\alpha$, even if they individually have lower posterior probability over $d$ than does $H_i^\alpha$, can act together to influence the classification of a new data point $y$. We can choose the lexicon in this example so as to showcase the largest possible effect these two subordinate rules could have by making the difference in consistent data between the (deterministic) hypotheses as small as possible, such that $H_i$ has a coverage advantage of only one data point over both $H_j$ and $H_k$. We will also consider those words for which $H_j$ and $H_k$ differ from the classification predicted by $H_i$ ($H_i(y)=c_1$), but agree with one another in selecting $c_2$ with the highest probability ($H_j(y)= H_k(y)= c_2$).

From Equation (2), with $G^*\text{-}P=1$,

$$p(H_{j/k}^\alpha \mid d) = \frac{\alpha}{1-2\alpha}\,p(H_i^\alpha \mid d) \qquad (4a)$$

Substituting (4a) into Equation (3) gives the probability that classification will occur in line with the dominant hypothesis $H_i$:

$$p(c_1 \mid d,y) = (1-2\alpha)P(H_i^\alpha \mid d) + \alpha\frac{\alpha}{1-2\alpha}P(H_i^\alpha \mid d) + \alpha\frac{\alpha}{1-2\alpha}P(H_i^\alpha \mid d) \qquad (4b)$$

And the probability that classification will occur in line with the subordinate, but mutually reinforcing, $H_j$ and $H_k$ can be calculated similarly.

The ratio of the probability of categorizing the new item consistently with $H_i$ to that of categorizing consistently with $H_j$ and $H_k$ can then be shown to be

$$\frac{p(c_1 \mid d,y)}{p(c_2 \mid d,y)} = \frac{6\alpha^2-4\alpha+1}{3\alpha(1-2\alpha)} \qquad (5)$$

Now take $H_i$ = *GUJARATI**, $H_j$= *GUJARATI*, and $H_k$ = *PENULT*; $y$ is a new word of the type in Row 4 of Table 1. The gang-up phenomenon, where *GUJARATI* and *PENULT* collude to move stress away from the position preferred by *GUJARATI**, may be seen to have any kind of appreciable effect (where $\frac{p(c_1 \mid d,y)}{p(c_2 \mid d,y)} \le 1.5$) only in the region $.17 < \alpha < .4$ (relatively large values for $\alpha$). Outside of this region *GUJARATI** dominates. And keep in mind, the advantage to *GUJARATI** only gets higher for larger differences in coverage (in Equation (5) only a single data point separates the three hypotheses), and for instances of lexical items where *GUJARATI* and *PENULT* disagree (Row 5 of Table 1).

So far we have seen that the Bayesian framework exhibits a potential over-sensitivity when applied to problems of the type formulated in this paper: learning over a space of quasi-categorical, contradictory hypotheses. This is true whether we consider learning to result in a single winner-take-all hypothesis, or instead opt for the weighted decision metric of the Optimal Bayes Classifier. We will return to this issue in Section 4. First, however, I will expand the hypothesis space under consideration, in Section 3.3, and introduce, in Section 3.4, a non-uniform prior, adding principled biases on the selection of those different hypotheses.

### 3.3 Mixed-Grammar Hypotheses

Before we can assess the performance of the Bayesian learner with respect to the UG-Delimited $\mathcal{H}$ Principle we must make sure we consider all potential competitor hypotheses that might be better predictors of the data than those examined so far. In particular, it is instructive to introduce something like a class of null hypotheses: hybrid grammars which explicitly encode equality between any pair of competing alternatives' ability to explain the data[5].

[5] The effect of mixed-grammar hypotheses can also be realized by allowing a selection procedure over a set of simple grammars, as described in Section 3.2, but, crucially, with the weights calculated under the assumption that data are generated by a combination of grammars (see, for example, the variational model proposed by Yang (1999), or the

I define this class as follows: the posterior probability that the hypothesis $\text{NULL}(i/j)^{\alpha}$ assigns to a stress class $c$ is calculated by allotting equal probability to selecting the $H_i^{\alpha}$ or the $H_j^{\alpha}$ rule to produce an output of that class:

$$p(c \mid NULL(i/j)^{\alpha}, y) = w_i p(c \mid H_i^{\alpha}, y) + w_j p(c \mid H_j^{\alpha}, y) \quad (6)$$

where $w_i = w_j = .5$. From Equation (6) and the definition in [3], we can compute the probability distribution of stress assignment $c$ given the application of $\text{NULL}(i/j)^{\alpha}$ to a particular word, $y$

[4] $\text{NULL}(i/j)^{\alpha}$: 'Null Hypothesis'

$$p(c \mid NULL(i/j)^{\alpha}, y) = \begin{cases} 1-2\alpha & c = H_i(y) = H_j(y) \\ \frac{1-\alpha}{2} & c = H_i(y)\ XOR\ c = H_j(y) \\ \alpha & c \neq H_i(y)\ \&\ c \neq H_j(y) \end{cases}$$

It can be shown that, for $L_{MU}'$ (the Gujarati′ lexicon generated from the Gujarati minimum uniform lexicon), the null hypothesis, $\text{NULL}(G^*/G)^{\alpha}$, is the decisive winner over $\text{GUJARATI}^{*\alpha}$ (by approximately 30 orders of magnitude). With this broader consideration of the hypothesis space, the anti-markedness grammar is no longer the outcome of learning. And it turns out that we can specify another hypothesis that gives an even higher likelihood over the data.

The 'maximum likelihood' hypotheses are specified by allowing all three parameters ($w_i$, $w_j$, and $\alpha$ (now $\sigma$)) in Equation (6) to be estimated from the data. $\text{MAX}(i/j)^{\sigma}$ is defined explicitly below in [5] for any given weighted combination of $H_i^{\sigma}$ and $H_j^{\sigma}$.

[5] $\text{MAX}(i/j)^{\sigma}$: 'Maximum Likelihood'

$$p(c \mid MAX(i/j)^{\sigma}, y) = \begin{cases} (w_i + w_j)(1-2\sigma) & c = H_i(y) = H_j(y) \\ (1-2\sigma)w_i + \sigma w_j & c = H_i(y)\ \&\ c \neq H_j(y) \\ (1-2\sigma)w_j + \sigma w_i & c = H_j(y)\ \&\ c \neq H_i(y) \\ (w_i + w_j)\sigma & c \neq H_i(y)\ \&\ c \neq H_j(y) \end{cases}$$

When $H_i$ = GUJARATI* and $H_j$ = GUJARATI, $\text{MAX}(G^*/G)^{\sigma}$ assigns the highest posterior of any we have seen so far (approximately 56 orders of magnitude larger than $G^*$). This is because, within the space of candidates, it gives the highest likelihood to the observed data, and the prior probability (assumed so far to be uniform) plays no role in this calculation. As the hypotheses we are considering become more complicated, however, we are led to consider an alternative to this assumption, one in which hypotheses with longer description lengths, or greater complexity, are penalized (Rissanen 1989).

probabilistic version of Optimality Theory over rankings utilized by Jarosz (2006)).

### 3.4 Non-Uniform Prior: Hypothesis Description Length

Under the uniform prior assumption, only with a lexicon in which GUJARATI* accounts for at least 44 times as much data as does GUJARATI will $\text{MAX}(G^*/G)^{\sigma}$ be defeated. In this section I will show how that result would be altered by considering a better approximation to the prior probability distribution over those hypotheses. $\text{MAX}(G^*/G)^{\sigma}$ and $\text{GUJARATI}^{*\alpha}$ can be seen to differ in a basic way related to the number of parameters and rules they must each keep track of. A domain-independent means of determining a prior probability based on this difference in size, or complexity, can be found in the information theoretic notion of coding cost, or description length.

Each hypothesis uses a particular labeling strategy to encode the input data (which can be quantified by the number of binary pieces of information, or bits needed to transmit that information to a waiting decoder). In addition, a certain number of bits is needed to encode the hypothesis itself. The total description length for a string (or set of data) $d$ and a particular hypothesis $H$ is given by the following general formula for two-part coding.

$$L(d,H) = L(d \mid H) + L(H) \quad (7)$$

The relation of (7) to Bayes Theorem becomes clear when we introduce the fundamental transformation from probability to optimal code length given by

$$L(x) = -\log P(x) \quad (8)$$

Intuitively, Equation (8) calls for assigning shorter length codes to higher probability symbols $x$ which, on average, will minimize the code length for a string, $d$, of symbols drawn from distribution $P(x)$. The ability to transform between length and probability allows for the conceptualization of the prior probabilities over the hypothesis space as biases against complexity.

We can think of the hypotheses in $\mathcal{H}$ as decision trees which produce stressed outputs from input words. In order to encode such decision trees we need something like the binary coding scheme given in Rissanen (1989, section 7.2).

$$L(T) = \log\binom{k_T + m_T - 2}{k_T} \quad (9)$$

Here $k_T$ is the number of internal (non-terminal) nodes in the tree and $m_T$ is the number of leaf (terminal) nodes. Equation (9) provides a measure of how much the grammar compresses its input – or how many classes it must keep track of to produce the correct output. For a series of decisions, based on querying for a series of features at a series of internal nodes, there will be a particular outcome at a particular leaf node. For the *GUJARATI** grammar, $k_T$=5 (corresponding to the relevant questions about vowel identity listed in definition [1] above), and $m_T$=6 (corresponding to the possible stress decisions resulting from the answers to each of those questions).

Additionally, all Non-Deterministic hypotheses require the estimation of at least one error term. I will approximate the coding length for a set of $k$ free parameters ($\hat{\theta}$), estimated over a string of length $n$, by Equation (10) (Rissanen 1989, section 3.1).

$$L(\hat{\theta}) = \frac{k}{2}\log n \quad (10)$$

Since I am only interested here in computing the length associated with the hypotheses themselves (the negative log of their prior probability), we will focus on the second term of Equation (7), which can be written as the sum of (9) and (10).

$MAX(G^*/G)^\sigma$ consists of a decision tree that is twice as large as that of $GUJARATI^{*\alpha}$ (since it keeps track of both $GUJARATI^{*\alpha}$ and $GUJARATI^{\alpha}$). Additionally, the combination hypothesis makes use of one more estimated parameter ($w_{G^*}$).

Under $L_{MU}'$, where $n$=512 words, the prior probability ratio[6] of $MAX(G^*/G)^\sigma$ to $GUJARATI^{*\alpha}$ is $1.7 \times 10^4$. From this result we can calculate that the type of lexicon in which the mixed-grammar hypothesis would be rejected is one in which the *GUJARATI** hypothesis accounts for at least eight times more data than does *GUJARATI* ($G^*/G = 8$).

This value must be regarded as an approximation due to its dependence on the particular coding scheme used[7]. It is, however, likely the best and most principled estimate of the linguistic-bias-free prior we can achieve[8].

Under the information theoretic treatment, its lower probability prior is still not enough to prevent $MAX(G^*/G)^\sigma$ from winning under $L_{MU}'$ (by 52 orders of magnitude over $GUJARATI^{*\alpha}$). The productions of a learner who has converged on this grammar would not be obviously consistent with a reversed sonority-to-stress output (since many words would show a stress pattern that is incompatible with that hypothesis), but neither would those productions be inconsistent with such a grammar (since a (slim) majority of words provide positive evidence for such a hypothesis). The typological status of such languages will be discussed in the following section.

## 4 Discussion & Conclusion

The foregoing analysis has served to address the question of whether the observed frequency of occurrence (approximately never) of anti-markedness systems (such as a grammar with a preference for stressing low sonority vowels over high) requires an active constraint that removes those grammars from the learner's hypothesis space. The central claim within this paper has been that attempts to answer this question must involve a careful examination and specification of the learning process, as well as the inputs to the learner.

Given that systems, at any particular time, tend

6 the contribution of the hypotheses lengths, converted back to probability via Equation (8)

7 In practice, a code length exactly equal to the negative log of the probability of a particular symbol may be unattainable, and the relationship in Equation (8) becomes an approximation which may be better in some cases than others. Due to this limitation, it is not clear how much the exact magnitude of a result obtained with this method can be relied upon (for a brief discussion of this issue see, for example, Brent (1999).)

8 An alternative to this approach is to imagine all grammars as potential mixtures, and to stipulate a prior probability distribution over the possible weight values. Each grammar in this view is equally complex, but certain weight combinations may be more likely than others (such as the 'simple' 0/100% distribution over weights). Conceptually this seems at least as reasonable as the current approach. We are still left, however, with the problem of determining the prior probability distribution over the weights, in a manner which, ideally, would be independent of the problem at hand.

to be in a state in which higher sonority vowels attract stress (due to assumed perceptual factors), the hypothetical sound change that disrupts the natural order must act over forms that are originally markedness-abiding. Thus, there will be a residue of those forms in the language even after the change has occurred (those in which /ə/'s *not* derived from /a/'s fail to attract stress in the presence of mid-sonority vowels). If this residue is small enough then the anti-markedness hypothesis might emerge as the winner. In turn, for this residue to be small, the lexicon before the change must exhibit a certain make-up, such that some word types either fail to appear or occur with much lower frequency than others.

In order to approximate these conditions I created 1000 (x5) simulated lexicons by sampling (without replacement) from the uniform word inventory ($L_{MU}$) at five different rates; for 3-syllable words: 1% (=5 types), 3% (=15 types), 5% (=26 types), 7% (=36 types), and 10% (=51 types). Higher sampling rates meant a greater likelihood of reproducing the underlying uniform type distribution over the 1000 trials, while lower sampling rates (under-sampling) allowed for a higher likelihood of departure from uniformity, and a greater chance for skewed, or outlier, lexicons to emerge.

These simulations were done for the full set of both 3-syllable and 2-syllable words (a more realistic distribution of input to the learner). To combine the two word lengths, with differing numbers of types, I scaled selection from the two classes. A cursory examination of the online English database CELEX (1993) gives a count of 45,652 for 3-syllable words, and 61,738 for 2-syllable words, a 1:1.4 relationship. Using this as a rough guide, and since the ratio of total types between 3-syllable and 2-syllable words is 512:64, a 1:10 scale was used (giving a proportion of 512:640=1:1.25). Each of the five sampling rates maintained this 1:10 scaling factor, such that the lexicon containing 3-syllable word types sampled at 7%, also contained 2-syllable word types sampled at 70%; this is the lexicon of 36 3-syllable word types (out of a possible total of 512) and 45 2-syllable word types (out of a possible total of 64) (Row 5: [36,45] in Table 2).

Each lexicon, $L$, at a particular sampling rate, was transformed to its $L'$ counterpart (via the change a>ə), and the coverage ratio between hypotheses *GUJARATI** and *GUJARATI* over $L'$ was computed. As given at the end of Section 3.4 for the description-length prior, a value greater than $G^*/G = 8$ is needed for a *GUJARATI** outcome. Here, due to concerns about the sensitivity of the Bayesian learner, and the degree of uncertainty in the calculation of the prior, I relax this criterion. The last four columns of Table 2 correspond to four (largely arbitrary) values for the $G^*/G$ ratio which were stipulated as thresholds (or possible prior probability ratios) that would allow *GUJARATI** to beat $MAX(G^*/G)^{\sigma}$. Each cell contains the percentage of anti-markedness outcomes (calculated from 1000 runs) for a given threshold, at a given sampling rate.

| Sampling Rate | [3,2]-syllable word types | G*/G 5 | 2.5 | 1.7 | 1.25 |
|---|---|---|---|---|---|
| 1%,10% | [5,6] | 0 | 0 | .4% | 6.4% |
| 3%,30% | [15,19] | 0 | 0 | 0 | .9% |
| 5%,50% | [26,32] | 0 | 0 | 0 | .1% |
| 7%,70% | [36,45] | 0 | 0 | 0 | 0 |
| 10%,100% | [51,64] | 0 | 0 | 0 | 0 |

Table 2: Estimated probabilities of learned anti-markedness grammar: under 5 different sampling rates (given as [number of 3-syllable,2-syllable word types]), for four different threshold coverage ratios.

The very low occurrence rates of Table 2 show that changing our assumptions about the make-up of the lexicon (departing from uniformity) do not qualitatively alter the results of the previous sections. A pure anti-markedness grammar (*GUJARATI**) seems to be a relatively rare outcome as compared to a mixed-grammar competitor ($MAX(G^*/G)^{\sigma}$), even under relaxed acceptance criteria.

The above work relies heavily on the existence of a residue of natural patterns in a post-sound change language. Under circumstances in which sound change is non-neutralizing (that is, ə is absent from the inventory of Gujarati before the sound change), there will be no contradictory evidence to the learner of Gujarati': all data is consistent with the *GUJARATI** hypothesis. Furthermore, there is a long-standing intuition in the literature that the most likely sound changes might actually be of this type (Martinet 1955)[9].

Under these circumstances we might expect *GUJARATI** to emerge as the clear winner. This will depend critically on whether or not we consider the lack of conflicting data to be an overwhelming factor in hypothesis selection. If, instead, we maintain our space of non-deterministic hypotheses, then there is still competition from the mixed-grammar alternatives. Under the non-neutralizing scenario, Gujarati has 7 vowels (rather than 8); for 3-syllable words, all 343 types support the $GUJARATI^{*\alpha}$ hypothesis, while 265 are also consistent with $PENULT^{\alpha}$. And $G*/P$ = 1.3. 2-syllable words will provide somewhat less of an advantage to the anti-markedness grammar (49:46~1.13), and with a larger weight (10 times greater frequency to approximate the CELEX ratios), giving an adjusted ratio of roughly 1.15. Whether this is enough of an advantage to cause *GUJARATI** to be selected will depend on the parameters of our learner, as well as the prior probability ratio between the two hypotheses: the difference in complexity between the *GUJARATI** rule, which computes stress location based on both position and sonority, and the *PENULT* rule, which only computes over position.

What the above discussion illustrates is that the actual form of common or likely sound changes can significantly alter the outcome of analysis. If non-neutralizing sound changes are the norm, then the dispreferred grammar might have a higher predicted likelihood than that calculated here. Alternatively, if chain shifts predominate, whereby all the vowels in the system undergo related incremental changes in quality, the outcome might be different again. And if realistic sound changes operate on a word by word basis, as predicted by Evolutionary Phonology, such that results are even less consistent in terms of sonority class, an even lower likelihood for a true anti-markedness grammar might be the result[10].

This work has been a preliminary attempt to accurately lay out the methodological requirements for addressing questions of how grammars arise. Further research ought to be concerned with exactly the complications to the question just raised. For present purposes, however, there are two general points to be made. The first is that, in order to determine what any theory predicts in this domain, one has to make assumptions about what constitutes a realistic language learner, as well as establish estimates of the normal state of lexical statistics. The second point is that determining those predictions tells us what the relevant typological facts are. The work here suggests that it is the occurrence, not so much of pure anti-markedness systems, but of partial anti-markedness (mixed-grammar) systems that is the critical issue. It may turn out to be the case that these systems are also very rare, and the over-prediction claim holds in its revised form. However, the true distribution of these types of languages seems far from clear at the present time, and work will have to be done to establish the fact of the matter[11].

## Acknowledgments

This work was supported by an NSF IGERT grant and a Department of Education Javits Fellowship. I would like to thank Paul Smolensky, Colin Wilson, and Simon Fischer-Baum for their invaluable assistance. Thanks also go to the three reviewers of this paper, especially Adam Albright for his extensive and extremely helpful comments.

[9] Thanks to Adam Albright for bringing this to my attention.

[10] Another issue so far undiscussed is the aptness of describing the *GUJARATI** hypothesis as a reversed sonority-to-stress scale. In either instantiation of Gujarati′ (deriving either from the 7- or 8-vowel system) there are only two operable sonority categories {MID,ə}. Stressing ə preferentially over a higher-sonority mid vowel is already dispreferred behavior from a universalist perspective, but it is qualitatively different than a hypothesis that targets sonority as the deciding factor (rather than vowel identity). This second hypothesis, for example, would avoid stressing newly encountered a's, precisely because of the high sonority of the vowel. The likelihood of achieving a true sonority scale reversal seems even lower than that of learning the 'stress-ə' rule. This is because the strongest evidence for a sonority-sensitive scale involves multiple tiers or classes of sonority (probably at least three). However, the more different classes of vowels (the more complications to the calculation of stress) the less likely it seems that an indirect sound change (one that does not target sonority itself) will produce a clean reversal of the pattern. Again, disorder, or proliferating 'co-phonologies' seem more likely to carry the day.

[11] In the first place, it is not a given that pure anti-markedness systems are completely non-occurring (see, for example, Poppe (1960); McLendon (1975); Breen and Pensalfini (1999)). As for potential mixed-grammar languages, these might include systems that have been analyzed as exhibiting high degrees of lexical exceptionality, or gone largely unanalyzed due to what is perceived as patternless behavior.

## References


Blevins, J. (2004). Evolutionary Phonology: the emergence of sound patterns. New York, Cambridge University Press.

Breen, G. and R. Pensalfini (1999). "Arrernte: a language with no syllable onsets." Linguistic Inquiry 30(1): 1-25.

Chater, N., J. B. Tenenbaum, et al. (2006). "Probabilistic models of cognition: conceptual foundations." Trends in Cognitive Science 10(7): 287-291.

Court, C. (1970). Nasal harmony and some indonesian sound laws. Pacific Linguistics Series C No.13. S. A. Wurm and C. Laycock.

de Lacy, P. (2006). Markedness: Reduction and Preservation in Phonology, Cambridge University Press.

Inkelas, S. (1997). The theoretical status of morphologically conditioned phonology: a case study of dominance effects. Yearbook of Morphology. G. Booij and J. van Marle, Kluwer Academic Publishers: 121-155.

Ito, J. and A. Mester (2001). "Covert generalizations in Optimality Theory: the role of stratal faithfulness constraints." Studies in Phonetics, Phonology and Morphology 7: 273-299.

Jarosz, G. (2006). Richness of the base and probabilistic unsupervised learning in Optimality Theory. Proceedings of the Eighth Meeting of the ACL Special Interest Group in Computational Phonology and Morphology, New York City.

Kemp, C., A. Perfors, et al. (2007). "Learning overhypotheses with hierarchical Bayesian models." Developmental Science 10(3): 307-321.

Kiparsky, P. (2004). "Universals constrain change; change results in typological generalizations." ms.

Kiparsky, P. (2006). "The Amphichronic Program vs. Evolutionary Phonology." Theoretical Linguistics 32: 217-236.

Kording, K. P. and D. M. Wolper (2006). "Bayesian decision theory in sensorimotor control." Trends in Cognitive Science 10(7): 319-326.

Martinet, A. (1955). Economie des changements phonetiques. Bern, Francke.

McLendon, S. (1975). A Grammar of Eastern Pomo, University of California Press.

Mitchell, T. M. (1997). Machine Learning, McGraw-Hill.

Pater, J. (2000). "Non-uniformity in English seconday stress: the role of ranked and lexically specific constraints." Phonology 17: 237-274.

Poppe, N. N. (1960). Buriat Grammar, Indiana University Publications.

Prince, A. and P. Smolenksy (1993/2004). Optimality Theory, Blackwell Publishing.

Rissanen, J. (1989). Stochastic Complexity in Statistical Enquiry, World Scientific Publishing Co.

Tenenbaum, J. B., C. Kemp, et al. (2007). Theory-based Bayesian models of inductive reasoning. Inductive Reasoning. A. Feeney and E. Heit, Cambridge University Press.

Yang, C. (1999). A Selectionist Theory of Language Acquisition. 27th Annual Meeting of the Association for Computational Linguistics, College Park, MD.

# A Bayesian model of natural language phonology: generating alternations from underlying forms

**David Ellis**
de@cs.brown.edu
Brown University
Providence, RI 02912

## Abstract

A stochastic approach to learning phonology. The model presented captures 7-15% more phonologically plausible underlying forms than a simple majority solution, because it prefers "pure" alternations. It could be useful in cases where an approximate solution is needed, or as a seed for more complex models. A similar process could be involved in some stages of child language acquisition; in particular, early learning of phonotactics.

## 1 Introduction

Sound changes in natural language, such as stem variation in inflected forms, can be described as phonological processes. These are governed by a constraint hierarchy as in Optimality Theory (OT), or by a set of ordered rules. Both rely on a single lexical representation of each morpheme (i.e., its underlying form), and context-sensitive transformations to surface forms. Phonological changes often affect segments near morpheme boundaries, but can also apply over an entire prosodic word, as in vowel harmony.

It does not seem straightforward to incorporate context into a Bayesian model of phonology, although a clever solution may yet be found. A standard way of incorporating conditioning environments is to treat them as factors in a Gibbs model (Liang and Klein, 2007), but such models require an explicit calculation of the partition function. Unless the rule contexts possess some kind of locality, we don't know how to compute this partition function efficiently. Some context could be captured by generating underlying phonemes from an n-gram model, or by annotating surface forms with neighborhood features. However, the effects of autosegmental phonology and other long-range dependencies (like vowel harmony) cannot be easily Bayesianized.

### 1.1 Related Work

In the last decade, finite-state approaches to phonology (Gildea and Jurafsky, 1996; Beesley and Karttunen, 2000) have effectively brought theoretical linguistic work on rewrite rules into the computational realm. A finite-state approximation of optimality theory (Karttunen, 1998) was later refined into a compact treatment of gradient constraints (Gerdemann and van Noord, 2000).

Recent work on Bayesian models of morphological segmentation (Johnson et al., 2007) could be combined with phonological rule induction (Goldwater and Johnson, 2004) in a variety of ways, some of which will be explored in our discussion of future work. Also, the Hierarchical Bayes Compiler (Daume III, 2007) could be used to generate a model similar to the one presented here, but less constrained[1] which makes correspondingly more random, less accurate predictions.

### 1.2 Dataset

As we describe the model and its implementation in this and subsequent sections, we will refer to a sam-

[1]Recent updates to HBC, inspired by discussions with the author, have addressed some of these limitations.



*Proceedings of the Tenth Meeting of the ACL Special Interest Group on Computational Morphology and Phonology*, pages 12–19,
Columbus, Ohio, USA June 2008. 

ple dataset (in Figure 1), consisting of a paradigm[2] of verb stems and person/number suffixes. The head of each row or column is an /underlying/ form, which in 3rd person singular is a phonologically null segment (represented as /ø/). In [surface] forms, the realization of each morpheme is affected by phonological processes. For example, in the combination of /tietä/ + /vat/, the result is [tietä+vät], where the 3rd person plural /a/ becomes [ä] due to vowel harmony.

### 1.3 Bayesian Approach

As a baseline model, we select the most frequently occurring allophone as the underlying form. Our goal is to outperform this baseline using a Bayesian model. In other words, what patterns in phonological processes can be inferred with such a statistical model? This simple framework begins learning with the assumption that the underlying forms are faithful to the surface (i.e., without considering markedness or phonotactics).

We model the generation of surface forms from underlying ones on the segmental (character) level. Input is an inflectional paradigm, with tokens of the form `stem+suffix`. Morphology is limited to a single suffix (no agglutination), and is already identified. Each character of an underlying stem or suffix ($u_i$) generates surface characters ($s_{ij}$) in an entire row or column of the input.

To capture the phonology of a variety of languages with a single model, we need constraints from linguistically plausible priors (universal grammar). We prefer that underlying characters be preserved in surface forms, especially when there is no alternation. It is also reasonable that there be fewer underlying forms (phonemes) than surface forms (phones, phonetic inventory), to account for allophones. We expect to be able to capture a significant subset of phonological processes using a simple model (only faithfulness constraints).

### 1.4 Pure Generators

Our model has an advantage over the baseline in its preference for "purity" in underlying forms. Each underlying segment should generate as few distinct surface segments as possible: if it generates non-alternating (identical) segments, it will be less likely to generate an alternation in addition. This means that when two segments alternate, the underlying form should be the one that appears less frequently in other contexts, irrespective of the majority within the alternation.

In the first stem of our Finnish verb conjugation (Figure 1), we see a [t,d] alternation (a case of consonant gradation), as well as unalternating [t]. If we isolate three of the surface forms where /tietä/ is inflected (1st person singular, and 3rd person singular and plural), and consider only the dental segments in the stem of each, we have two underlying segments. Here, we use question marks to indicate unknown underlying segments.

/??/ [dt] [tt] [tt]

In this subset of the data, the reasonable candidate underlying forms are /t/ and /d/. These two compete to explain the observed data (surface forms). The nature of the prior probability distribution determines whether the majority is hypothesized for each underlying form, so /t/ produces both alternating and unalternating surface segments, or /d/ is hypothesized as the source of the alternation (and /t/ remains "pure"). In a Bayesian setting, we impose a sparse prior over underlying forms conditioned on the surface forms they generate.

If $u_2$ is hypothesized to be /t/, the posterior probability of $u_1$ being /t/ goes down:

$$P(u_1 = /t/|u_2 = /t/) < P(u_1 = /t/)$$

The probability of $u_1$ being the competitor, /d/, correspondingly increases:

$$P(u_1 = /d/|u_2 = /t/) > P(u_1 = /d/)$$

Even though the majority in this case would be /t/, the favored candidate for the alternating form was /d/. This happened because of how we defined the model's prior, in combination with the evidence that /t/ (assigned to $u_2$) generated the sequence of [t]. So selection bias prefers /d/ as the source of an ambiguous segment, leaving /t/ to always generate itself.

A similar effect can occur if there are both unalternating [t]'s and [d]'s on the surface, in addition to the [t,d] alternation. The candidate (/t/ or /d/) that is

[2]The paradigm format lends itself to analysis of word types, but if supplemented with surface counts, can also handle tokens.

| Stem \ Suffix | /n/ (1s) | /t/ (2s) | /ø/ (3s) | /mme/ (1p) | /tte/ (2p) | /vat/ (3p) |
|---|---|---|---|---|---|---|
| /tietä/ | [tiedä+n] | [tiedä+t] | [tietä+ä] | [tiedä+mme] | [tiedä+tte] | [tietä+vät] |
| /aiko/ | [aiøo+n] | [aiøo+t] | [aiko+o] | [aiøo+mme] | [aiøo+tte] | [aiko+vat] |
| /luke/ | [luøe+n] | [luøe+t] | [luke+e] | [luøe+mme] | [luøe+tte] | [luke+vat] |
| /puhu/ | [puhu+n] | [puhu+t] | [puhu+u] | [puhu+mme] | [puhu+tte] | [puhu+vat] |
| /saa/ | [saa+n] | [saa+t] | [saa+ø] | [saa+mme] | [saa+tte] | [saa+vat] |
| /tule/ | [tule+n] | [tule+t] | [tule+e] | [tule+mme] | [tule+tte] | [tule+vat] |
| /pelkää/ | [pelkää+n] | [pelkää+t] | [pelkää+ø] | [pelkää+mme] | [pelkää+tte] | [pelkää+vät] |

Figure 1: Sample dataset (constructed by hand): Finnish verbs, with inflection for person and number.

generating fewer unalternating segments is preferred to explain the alternation. For example, if there were 1000 cases of [t], 500 [d] and 500 [t,d], we would expect the following hypotheses: $/t/ \rightarrow [t]$, $/d/ \rightarrow [d]$ and $/d/ \rightarrow [t, d]$. This is because one of the two candidates must be responsible for both unalternating and alternating segments, but we prefer to have as much "'purity" as possible, to minimize ambiguity.

With this solution, we still have 1000 pure $/t/ \rightarrow [t]$, and only the 500 $/d/ \rightarrow [d]$ are now indistinct from $/d/ \rightarrow [t, d]$. If we had selected /t/ as the source of the alternation, there would be only 500 remaining "pure" (/d/) segments, and 1500 ambiguous $/t/$. Our Bayesian model should prefer the less ambiguous ("purer") solution, given an appropriate prior.

## 2 Model

We will use boldface to indicate vectors, and subscripts to identify an element from a vector or matrix. The variable $\mathbf{N}(\mathbf{u})$ is a vector of observed counts with the current underlying form hypotheses. The notation we use for a vector $\mathbf{u}$ with one element $i$ removed is $\mathbf{u}_{-i}$, so we can exclude the counts associated with a particular underlying form by indicating that in the parenthesized variable (i.e., $\mathbf{N}(\mathbf{u}_{-4})$ is all the counts except those associated with the fourth underlying form). $N_i(\mathbf{u})$ is the number of times character $i$ is used as an underlying form, and $N_{ij}(\mathbf{u})$ is the number of times character $i$ generated surface character $j$.

The priors over surface $\mathbf{s}$ and underlying $\mathbf{u}$ segments in Figure 2 are captured by Dirichlet priors $\boldsymbol{\alpha}$ and $\boldsymbol{\beta}$, which generate the multinomial distributions $\boldsymbol{\theta}$ and $\boldsymbol{\phi}$, respectively (see Figure 3). The prior over underlying form encourages sparse solutions, so $\beta_u < 1$ for all $u$. The prior over surface form given underlying encourages identity mapping, $/x/ \rightarrow [x]$, so $\alpha_{xx} > 1$, and discourages different segments, $/x/ \rightarrow [y]$, so $\alpha_{xy} < 1$ for all $x \neq y$.

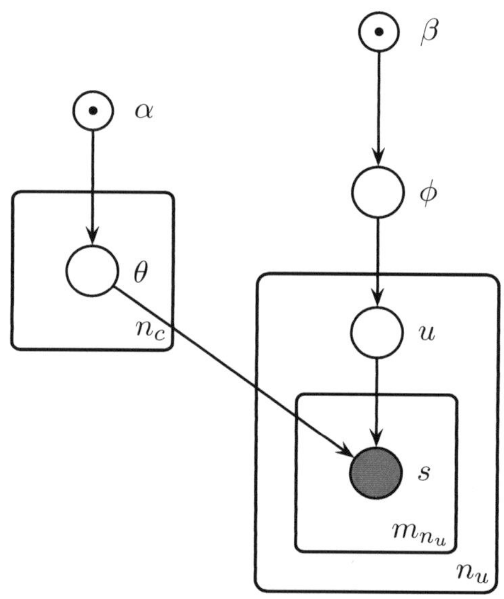


Figure 2: Bayesian network: $\boldsymbol{\alpha}$ and $\boldsymbol{\beta}$ are vectors of hyperparameters, and $\boldsymbol{\theta}_i$ (for $i \in \{1, \ldots, n_c\}$) and $\boldsymbol{\phi}$ are distributions. $\mathbf{u}$ is a vector of underlying forms, generated from $\boldsymbol{\phi}$, and $\mathbf{s}_i$ (for $i \in n_u$) is a set of observed surface forms generated from the hidden variable $u_i$ according to $\boldsymbol{\theta}_i$

Phones and phonemes are drawn from a set of characters (e.g., IPA, unicode) $C$ used to represent them. $\phi_i$ is the probability of a character ($C_i$ for $i \in n_c$) being an underlying form, irrespective of current alignments or its position in the paradigm. $\theta_{ij}$ is the conditional probability of a surface char-

$$
\begin{array}{llll}
\boldsymbol{\theta}_c & | \; \boldsymbol{\alpha} & \sim & \text{DIR}(\boldsymbol{\alpha}), c = 1, \ldots, n_c \\
\boldsymbol{\phi} & | \; \boldsymbol{\beta} & \sim & \text{DIR}(\boldsymbol{\beta}) \\
u_i & | \; \boldsymbol{\phi}_i & \sim & \text{MULTI}(\boldsymbol{\phi}_i), i = 1, \ldots, n_u \\
s_{ij} & | \; u_i, \boldsymbol{\theta}_{u_i} & \sim & \text{MULTI}(\boldsymbol{\theta}_{u_i}), i = 1, \ldots, n_u, \\
 & & & \quad j = 1, \ldots, m_i
\end{array}
$$

Figure 3: Model parameters: $n_c$ is # different segments, $n_u$ is # underlying segments

acter ($s_{kn} = C_j$ for $j \in n_c$, $n \in m_k$) given the underlying character it is generated from ($u_k = C_i$ for $i \in n_c$, $k \in n_u$), which is determined by its position in the paradigm.

In our Finnish example (Figure 1), if $k = 1$, we are looking at the first underlying character, which is /t/ (from /tietä/), so assuming our character set is the Finnish alphabet, of which 't' is the 20th character, $u_1 = C_{20} =$ t. It generates the first character of each inflected form (1st, 2nd, 3rd person, singular and plural) of that stem, so $m_1 = 6$, and since there is no alternation $s_{1n} =$ t (for $n \in \{1, \ldots, 6\}$). Given the phonologically plausible (gold) underlying forms, the probability of /t/ is $\phi_{20} = 7/41$.

On the other hand, $k = 33$ identifies the 3rd person singular /ø/, which inflects each of the seven stems, so $m_{33} = 7$. Since we need our alphabet to identify a null character, we'll give it index zero (i.e., $u_{33} = C_0 = \emptyset$). For each of the (underlying, surface) alignments in this alternation (caused by vowel gemination), we can identify the probability in $\boldsymbol{\theta}$. For 3rd person singular [tietä+ä], where $s_{33,1} = C_{28} =$ ä, the conditional probability $\theta_{0,28} = 1/7$.

The prior hyperparameters can be understood as follows. As $\beta_i$ gets smaller, an underlying form $u_k$ is less likely to be $C_i$. As $\alpha_{ij}$ gets smaller, an underlying $u_k = C_i$ is less likely to generate a surface segment $s_{kn} = C_j \; \forall n \in m_k$. In our experiments, we will vary $\alpha_{i=j}$ (prior over identity map from underlying to surface) and $\alpha_{i \neq j}$.

Our implementation of this model uses Gibbs sampling (c.f., (Bishop, 2006), pp 542-8), an algorithm that produces samples from the posterior distribution. Each sample is an assignment of the hidden variables, **u** (i.e., a set of hypothesized underlying forms). Our sampler initializes **u** from a uniform distribution over segments in the training data, and resamples underlying forms in a fixed order, as input in the paradigm. Rather than reestimate $\boldsymbol{\theta}$ and $\boldsymbol{\phi}$ at each iteration before sampling from **u**, we can marginalize these intermediate probability distributions in order to ease implementation and speed convergence.

Our search procedure tries to sample from the posterior probability, according to Bayes' rule.

$$\text{posterior} \propto \text{likelihood} * \text{prior}$$

$$P(\mathbf{u}, \mathbf{s} | \boldsymbol{\beta}, \boldsymbol{\alpha}) \propto P(\mathbf{u} | \boldsymbol{\beta}) P(\mathbf{s}, \mathbf{u} | \boldsymbol{\alpha})$$

Each of these probabilities is drawn from a Dirichlet distribution, which is defined in terms of the multivariate Beta function, $C$. The prior $\boldsymbol{\beta}$ added to underlying counts $\mathbf{N}(\mathbf{u})$ forms the posterior Dirichlet corresponding to $P(\mathbf{u}|\boldsymbol{\beta})$. In $P(\mathbf{s}|\mathbf{u}, \boldsymbol{\alpha})$, each $\boldsymbol{\alpha}_i$ vector is supplemented by the observed counts of (underlying, surface) pairs $N(\mathbf{s}_i)$.

$$P(\mathbf{u}, \mathbf{s} | \boldsymbol{\beta}, \boldsymbol{\alpha}) = \frac{C(\boldsymbol{\beta} + N(\mathbf{u}))}{C(\boldsymbol{\beta})} \prod_{c=1}^{n_c} \frac{C(\boldsymbol{\alpha}_c + \sum_{i:u_i=c} N(\mathbf{s}_i))}{C(\boldsymbol{\alpha})}$$

The collapsed update procedure consists of resampling each underlying form, $u$, incorporating the prior hyperparameters $\boldsymbol{\alpha}, \boldsymbol{\beta}$ and counts $N$ over the rest of the dataset. The relevant counts for a candidate $k$ being the underlying form $u_i$ are $N_k(\mathbf{u}_{-i})$ and $N_{ks_{ij}}(\mathbf{u}_{-i})$ for $j \in m_i$. $P(u_i = k | \mathbf{u}_{-i}, \boldsymbol{\alpha}, \boldsymbol{\beta})$ is proportional to the probability of generating $u_i = k$, given the other $\mathbf{u}_{-i}$ and all $s_{ij}$ (for $j \in m_i$), given $\mathbf{s}_{-i}$ and $\mathbf{u}_{-i}$.

$$P(u_i = c | \mathbf{u}_{-i}, \boldsymbol{\alpha}, \boldsymbol{\beta}) \propto \frac{N_c(u_{-i}) + \boldsymbol{\beta}_c}{n - 1 + \boldsymbol{\beta}_\bullet} \frac{C(\boldsymbol{\alpha} + \sum_{i' \neq i : u_{i'} = c} N(s'_i) + N(s_i))}{C(\boldsymbol{\alpha} + \sum_{i' \neq i : u_{i'} = c} N(s'_i))}$$

Suppose we were updating this sampler running on the Finnish verb inflections. If we had all segments as in Figure 1, but wanted to resample $u_{31}$ (1st person singular /n/), we would consider the counts $N$ excluding that form (i.e., under $\mathbf{u}_{-31}$). The prior for /n/, $\beta_{14}$, is fixed, and there are no other occurrences, so $N_{14}(\mathbf{u}_{-31}) = 0$. Another potential underlying form, like /t/, would have higher unconditioned posterior probability, because of the counts

(7, in this case) added to its prior from $\boldsymbol{\beta}$. Then, we have to multiply by the probability of each generated surface segment (all are [n], so $7 * P([n]|c, \boldsymbol{\alpha})$ for a given hypothesis $u_{31} = c$).

We select a given character $c \in C$ for $u_{31}$ from a distribution at random. Depending on the prior, /n/ will be the most likely choice, but other values are still possible with smaller probability. The counts used for the next resampling, $N(\mathbf{u}_{-31})$, are affected by this choice, because the new identity of $u_{31}$ has contributed to the posterior distribution. After unbounded iterations, Gibbs sampling is guaranteed to converge and produce samples from the true posterior (Geman and Geman, 1984).

## 3 Evaluation

This model provides a language agnostic solution to a subset of phonological problems. We will first examine performance on the sample Finnish data (from Figure 1), and then look more closely at the issue of convergence. Finally, we present results from larger corpora [3].

### 3.1 Finnish

Output from a trial run on Finnish verbs (from Figure 1) follows, with hyperparameters $\alpha_{ij}\{100 \iff i = j, 0.05 \iff i \neq j\}$ and $\beta_i = \{0.1\}$.

In the paradigm (a sample after 1000 iterations), each [sur+face] form is followed by its hypothesized /under/ + /lying/ morphemes.

[tiedä+n] : /tiedä/ + /n/
[tiedä+t] : /tiedä/ + /t/
[tietä+ä] : /tiedä/ + /ä/
[tiedä+mme] : /tiedä/ + /mme/
[tiedä+tte] : /tiedä/ + /tte/
[tietä+vät] : /tiedä/ + /vät/
[aiøo+n] : /aiøo/ + /n/
...
[pelkää+vät] : /pelkää/ + /vat/

With strong enough priors (faithfulness constraints), our sampler often selects the most common surface form aligned with an underlying segment. Although [vat] is more common than [vät], we choose the latter as the purer underlying form. So /a/ is always [a], but /ä/ can be either [ä] or [a].

[3] 2.8 million word types from Morphochallenge2007 (Kurimo et al., 2007)

### 3.2 Convergence

Testing convergence, we run again on the sample data (Figure 1), using $\alpha_{ij} = 0.1$ when $i \neq j$ and 10 when $i = j$ and $\boldsymbol{\beta} = 0.1$, starting from different initializations, we get the same solution.

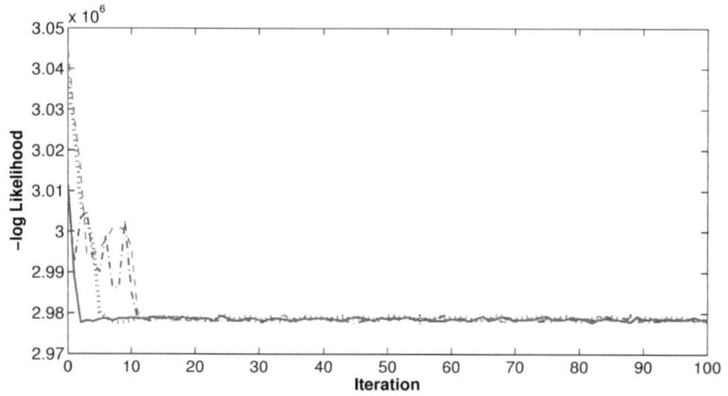


Figure 4: Posterior likelihood at each of the first 100 iterations, from 4 runs (with different random seeds) on 10% of the Morphochallenge dataset ($\alpha_{i \neq j} = 0.001, \alpha_{i=j} = 100, \beta = 0.1$), indicating convergence within the first 15 iterations.

To confirm that the sampler has converged, we output and plot trace statistics at each iteration, including marginal probability, log likelihood, and changes in underlying forms (i.e., variables resampled). If the sampler has converged, there should no longer be a trend (consistent slope) in any of these statistics (as in Figure 4).

Examining the posterior probability of each selected underlying form reveals interesting patterns that also help explain the variation. In the above run, the ambiguous segments (with surface alternations) were drawn from the distributions (with improbable segments elided) in Figure 5.

We expect this model to maximize the probability of either the "majority" solution or a solution demonstrating selection bias. We compare likelihood of the posterior sample with that of a "phonologically plausible" solution (in which underlying forms are determined by referring to formal linguistic accounts of phonological derivation) and a "majority solution" (see Figure 6 for a log-log plot, where lower is more likely).

The posterior sample has optimal likelihood with each parameter setting, as expected. The majority parse is selected with $\alpha_{i \neq j} = 0.5$ With lower values of $\alpha_{i \neq j}$, the "phonologically plausible" parse is

$u_4$=/d/ $s_4$=[d,d,t,d,d,t]
$P(u_i = c) \quad \approx$
d 0.99968
t 0.00014
$u_8$=/k/ $s_8$=[ø,ø,k,ø,ø,k]
(same behavior as $u_{12}$)
$P(u_i = c) \quad \approx$
ø 0.642
k 0.124
$u_{33}$=/e/ $s_{33}$=[ä,o,e,u,ø,e,ø]
$P(u_i = c) \quad \approx$
ä,o,u 0.0029
ø 0.215
a 0.0003
e 0.297

Figure 5: Resampling probabilities for alternations, after 1000 iterations.

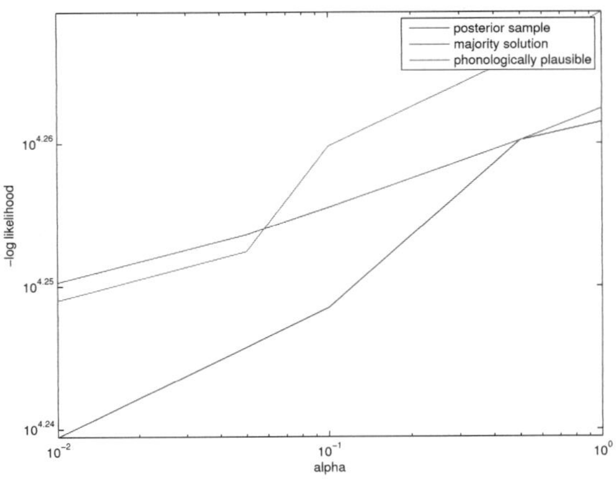


Figure 6: Parse likelihood

more likely than the majority. However, the sampler does not converge to this solution, because in this [t,d] alternation, the "phonologically plausible" solution identifies /t/, but neither selection bias nor majority rules would lead to that with the given data.

### 3.3 Morphologically segmented corpora

In our search for appropriate data for additional, larger-scale experiments, we found several viable alternatives. The correct morphological segmentations for Finnish data used in Morphochallenge2007 (Kurimo et al., 2007) provide a rich and varied set of words, and are readily analyzable by our sampler. Rather than associating each surface form with a position in the paradigm, we use the annotated morphemes.

| | Majority | Bayesian |
|---|---|---|
| types | 50.84 | 69.53 |
| tokens | 65.23 | 72.11 |

Figure 7: Accuracy of underlying segment hypotheses.

For example, the word *ajavalle* is listed in the corpus as follows:

ajavalle aja:ajaa|V va:PCP1 lle:ALL The word is segmented into a verb stem, 'aja' (drive), a present participle marker 'va', and the allative suffix ("for"). Each surface realization of a given morpheme is identified by the same tag (e.g., PCP1). However, in this corpus, insertion and deletion are not explicitly marked (as they were in the paradigm, by ø). Rather than introduce another component to determine which segments in the form were dropped, we ignore these cases.

The sampling algorithm proceeds as described in section 2. To run on tokens (as opposed to types), we incorporate another input file that contains counts from the original text (*ajavalle* appeared 8 times). The counts of each morpheme's surface forms then reflect the number of times that form appeared in any word in the corpus.

#### 3.3.1 Type or Token

In Finnish verb conjugation, 3rd person (esp. singular) forms have high frequency and tend to be unmarked (i.e., closer to underlying). In types, unmarked is a minority (one third), but incorporating token frequency shifts that balance, benefiting the "majority learner." Among noun inflections, unmarked has higher frequency in speech, but marked tokens may still dominate in text. We might expect that it is easier to learn from tokens than types, in part because more data is often helpful.

Testing on half of the Morphochallenge 2007 Finnish data (1M word types, 5M morph types, 17.5M word tokens, 48M morph tokens), we ran both our Bayesian model and a majority solver on the morphological analyses, and compared against phonologically plausible (gold) underlying forms. Results are reported in Figure 7.

The Bayesian estimate consistently outperformed the majority solution, and cases where the two differ could often be ascribed to the preference for "pure" analyses.

## 4 Conclusion

We have described a model where surface forms are generated from underlying representations segment by segment. Taking this approach allowed us to investigate the properties of a Bayesian statistical learner, and how these can be useful in the context of sound systems, a basic component of language. Experiments with our implementation of a collapsed sampler have produced results largely confirming our hypotheses.

Without context, we can often learn about 60 to 80 percent of the mapping from underlying phonemes to surface phones. Especially with lower values of $\alpha_{i \neq j}$, closer to 0, our model does prefer pure alternations. Gibbs sampling tends to select the majority underlying form, particularly with $\alpha_{i \neq j}$ relatively high, closer to 1. So, a sparser prior leads us further from the baseline, and often closer to a phonologically plausible solution.

### 4.1 Directions

In future research, we hope to integrate morphological analysis into this sort of a treatment of phonology. This is a natural approach for children learning their first language. They intuitively discover phonotactics, and how it affects the prosodic shape of each word, as they learn meaningful units and compose them together. It is clear that many layers of linguistic information interact in the early stages of child language acquisition (Demuth and Ellis, 2005 in press), so they should also interact in our models. As discussed above, the present model should be applicable to analysis of language-learners' speech errors, and this connection should be explored in greater depth.

It might be interesting to predispose the sampler to select underlying forms from open syllables. That is, set $\alpha$ to increase the probability of matching one of the surface segments if its context (feature annotations) includes a vocalic segment or a word boundary immediately following. The probability of phonological processes like assimilation could be similarly modeled, with the prior higher for choosing a segment that appears on the surface in a contrastive context (where it shares few features with neighboring segments).

If we define a MaxEnt distribution over Optimality Theoretic constraints, we might use that to inform our selection of underlying forms. In (Goldwater and Johnson, 2003), the learning algorithm was given a set of candidate surface forms associated with an underlying form, and tried to optimize the constraint weights. In addition to the constraint weights, we must also optimize the underlying form, since our goal is to take as input only observable data. Sampling from this type of complex distribution is quite difficult, but some approaches (e.g., (Murray et al., 2006)) may help reduce the intractability.

## References


Kenneth R. Beesley and Lauri Karttunen. 2000. Finite-state non-concatenative morphotactics. In Lauri Karttunen, Jason Eisner, and Alain Thériault, editors, *SIGPHON2000, August 6 2000. Proceedings of the Fifth Workshop of the ACL Special Interest Group in Computational Phonology.*, pages 1–12.

Christopher M. Bishop. 2006. *Pattern Recognition and Machine Learning (Information Science and Statistics).* Springer, August.

Hal Daume III. 2007. Hbc: Hierarchical bayes compiler.

Katherine Demuth and David Ellis, 2005 (in press). *Revisiting the acquisition of Sesotho noun class prefixes.* Lawrence Erlbaum.

Stuart Geman and Donald Geman. 1984. Stochastic relaxation, gibbs distributions, and the bayesian restoration of images. *IEEE Trans. Pattern Anal. Machine Intell.*, 6(6):721–741, Nov.

Dale Gerdemann and Gertjan van Noord. 2000. Approximation and exactness in finite state optimality theory.

Daniel Gildea and Daniel Jurafsky. 1996. Learning bias and phonological-rule induction. *Computational Linguistics*, 22(4):497–530.

Sharon Goldwater and Mark Johnson. 2003. Learning ot constraint rankings using a maximum entropy model.

Sharon Goldwater and Mark Johnson. 2004. Priors in Bayesian learning of phonological rules. In *Proceedings of the Seventh Meeting of the ACL Special Interest Group in Computational Phonology*, pages 35–42, Barcelona, Spain, July. Association for Computational Linguistics.

Mark Johnson, Thomas L. Griffiths, and Sharon Goldwater. 2007. Adaptor grammars: A framework for specifying compositional nonparametric Bayesian models. In B. Schölkopf, J. Platt, and T. Hoffman, editors, *Advances in Neural Information Processing Systems 19*, pages 641–648. MIT Press, Cambridge, MA.

Lauri Karttunen. 1998. The proper treatment of optimality in computational phonology. In Lauri Karttunen, editor, *FSMNLP'98: International Workshop on Finite State Methods in Natural Language Processing*, pages 1–12. Association for Computational Linguistics, Somerset, New Jersey.

Mikko Kurimo, Mathias Creutz, and Ville Turunen. 2007. Overview of morpho challenge in clef 2007. In *Working Notes for the CLEF 2007 Workshop*, Budapest, Hungary.

Percy Liang and Dan Klein. 2007. Tutorial 1: Bayesian nonparametric structured models, June.

Iain Murray, Zoubin Ghahramani, and David MacKay. 2006. MCMC for doubly-intractable distributions. In *UAI*. AUAI Press.

# Unsupervised word segmentation for Sesotho using Adaptor Grammars

**Mark Johnson**
Brown University
Mark_Johnson@Brown.edu

## Abstract

This paper describes a variety of non-parametric Bayesian models of word segmentation based on *Adaptor Grammars* that model different aspects of the input and incorporate different kinds of prior knowledge, and applies them to the Bantu language Sesotho. While we find overall word segmentation accuracies lower than these models achieve on English, we also find some interesting differences in which factors contribute to better word segmentation. Specifically, we found little improvement to word segmentation accuracy when we modeled contextual dependencies, while modeling morphological structure did improve segmentation accuracy.

## 1 Introduction

A Bayesian approach to learning (Bishop, 2006) is especially useful for computational models of language acquisition because we can use it to study the effect of different kinds and amounts of *prior knowledge* on the learning process. The Bayesian approach is agnostic as to what this prior knowledge might consist of; the prior could encode the kinds of rich universal grammar hypothesised by e.g., Chomsky (1986), or it could express a vague non-linguistic preference for simpler as opposed to more complex models, as in some of the grammars discussed below. Clearly there's a wide range of possible priors, and one of the exciting possibilities raised by Bayesian methods is that we may soon be able to empirically evaluate the potential contribution of different kinds of prior knowledge to language learning.

The Bayesian framework is surprisingly flexible. The bulk of the work on Bayesian inference is on *parametric models*, where the goal is to learn the value of a set of parameters (much as in Chomsky's Principles and Parameters conception of learning). However, recently Bayesian methods for *nonparametric inference* have been developed, in which the parameters themselves, as well as their values, are learned from data. (The term "nonparametric" is perhaps misleading here: it does not mean that the models have no parameters, rather it means that the learning process considers models with different sets of parameters). One can think of the prior as providing an infinite set of possible parameters, from which a learner selects a subset with which to model their language.

If one pairs each of these infinitely-many parameters with possible structures (or equivalently, rules that generate such structures) then these non-parametric Bayesian learning methods can learn the structures relevant to a language. Determining whether methods such as these can in fact learn linguistic structure bears on the nature vs. nurture debates in language acquisition, since one of the arguments for the nativist position is that there doesn't seem to be a way to learn structure from the input that children receive.

While there's no reason why these methods can't be used to learn the syntax and semantics of human languages, much of the work to date has focused on lower-level learning problems such as morphological structure learning (Goldwater et al., 2006b) and word segmentation, where the learner is given unsegmented broad-phonemic utterance transcriptions



*Proceedings of the Tenth Meeting of the ACL Special Interest Group on Computational Morphology and Phonology*, pages 20–27,
Columbus, Ohio, USA June 2008. 

and has to identify the word boundaries (Goldwater et al., 2006a; Goldwater et al., 2007). One reason for this is that these problems seem simpler than learning syntax, where the non-linguistic context plausibly supplies important information to human learners. Virtually everyone agrees that the set of possible morphemes and words, if not infinite, is astronomically large, so it seems plausible that humans use some kind of nonparametric procedure to learn the lexicon.

Johnson et al. (2007) introduced *Adaptor Grammars* as a framework in which a wide variety of linguistically-interesting nonparametric inference problems can be formulated and evaluated, including a number of variants of the models described by Goldwater (2007). Johnson (2008) presented a variety of different adaptor grammar word segmentation models and applied them to the problem of segmenting Brent's phonemicized version of the Bernstein-Ratner corpus of child-directed English (Bernstein-Ratner, 1987; Brent, 1999). The main results of that paper were the following:

1. it confirmed the importance of modeling contextual dependencies above the word level for word segmentation (Goldwater et al., 2006a),
2. it showed a small but significant improvement to segmentation accuracy by learning the possible syllable structures of the language together with the lexicon, and
3. it found no significant advantage to learning morphological structure together with the lexicon (indeed, that model confused morphological and lexical structure).

Of course the last result is a null result, and it's possible that a different model would be able to usefuly combine morphological learning with word segmentation.

This paper continues that research by applying the same kinds of models to Sesotho, a Bantu language spoken in Southern Africa. Bantu languages are especially interesting for this kind of study, as they have rich productive agglutinative morphologies and relatively transparent phonologies, as compared to languages such as Finnish or Turkish which have complex harmony processes and other phonological complexities. The relative clarity of Bantu has inspired previous computational work, such as the algorithm for learning Swahili morphology by Hu et al. (2005). The Hu et al. algorithm uses a Minimum Description Length procedure (Rissanen, 1989) that is conceptually related to the nonparametric Bayesian procedure used here. However, the work here is focused on determining whether the word segmentation methods that work well for English generalize to Sesotho and whether modeling morphological and/or syllable structure improves Sesotho word segmentation, rather than learning Sesotho morphological structure per se.

The rest of this paper is structured as follows. Section 2 informally reviews adaptor grammars and describes how they are used to specify different Bayesian models. Section 3 describes the Sesotho corpus we used and the specific adaptor grammars we used for word segmentation, and section 5 summarizes and concludes the paper.

## 2 Adaptor grammars

One reason why Probabilistic Context-Free Grammars (PCFGs) are interesting is because they are very simple and natural models of hierarchical structure. They are parametric models because each PCFG has a fixed number of rules, each of which has a numerical parameter associated with it. One way to construct nonparametric Bayesian models is to take a parametric model class and let one or more of their components grow unboundedly.

There are two obvious ways to construct nonparametric models from PCFGs. First, we can let the number of nonterminals grow unboundedly, as in the *Infinite PCFG*, where the nonterminals of the grammar can be indefinitely refined versions of a base PCFG (Liang et al., 2007). Second, we can fix the set of nonterminals but permit the number of rules or productions to grow unboundedly, which leads to Adaptor Grammars (Johnson et al., 2007).

At any point in learning, an Adaptor Grammar has a finite set of rules, but these can grow unboundedly (typically logarithmically) with the size of the training data. In a word-segmentation application these rules typically generate words or morphemes, so the learner is effectively learning the morphemes and words of its language.

The new rules learnt by an Adaptor Grammar are

compositions of old ones (that can themselves be compositions of other rules), so it's natural to think of these new rules as tree fragments, where each entire fragment is associated with its own probability. Viewed this way, an adaptor grammar can be viewed as learning the tree fragments or constructions involved in a language, much as in Bod (1998). For computational reasons adaptor grammars require these fragments to consist of subtrees (i.e., their yields are terminals).

We now provide an informal description of Adaptor Grammars (for a more formal description see Johnson et al. (2007)). An adaptor grammar consists of terminals $V$, nonterminals $N$ (including a start symbol $S$), initial rules $R$ and rule probabilities $p$, just as in a PCFG. In addition, it also has a vector of *concentration parameters* $\boldsymbol{\alpha}$, where $\alpha_A \geq 0$ is called the *(Dirichlet) concentration parameter* associated with nonterminal $A$.

The nonterminals $A$ for which $\alpha_A > 0$ are *adapted*, which means that each subtree for $A$ that can be generated using the initial rules $R$ is considered as a potential rule in the adaptor grammar. If $\alpha_A = 0$ then $A$ is *unadapted*, which means it expands just as in an ordinary PCFG.

Adaptor grammars are so-called because they adapt both the subtrees and their probabilities to the corpus they are generating. Formally, they are Hierarchical Dirichlet Processes that generate a distribution over distributions over trees that can be defined in terms of stick-breaking processes (Teh et al., 2006). It's probably easiest to understand them in terms of their conditional or sampling distribution, which is the probability of generating a new tree $T$ given the trees $(T_1, \ldots, T_n)$ that the adaptor grammar has already generated.

An adaptor grammar can be viewed as generating a tree top-down, just like a PCFG. Suppose we have a node $A$ to expand. If $A$ is unadapted (i.e., $\alpha_A = 0$) then $A$ expands just as in a PCFG, i.e., we pick a rule $A \rightarrow \beta \in R$ with probability $p_{A \rightarrow \beta}$ and recursively expand $\beta$. If $A$ is adapted and has expanded $n_A$ times before, then:

1. $A$ expands to a subtree $\sigma$ with probability $n_\sigma/(n_A + \alpha_A)$, where $n_\sigma$ is the number of times $A$ has expanded to subtree $\sigma$ before, and
2. $A$ expands to $\beta$ where $A \rightarrow \beta \in R$ with probability $\alpha_A \, p_{A \rightarrow \beta}/(n_A + \alpha_A)$.

Thus an adapted nonterminal $A$ expands to a previously expanded subtree $\sigma$ with probability proportional to the number $n_\sigma$ of times it was used before, and expands just as in a PCFG (i.e., using $R$) with probability proportional to the concentration parameter $\alpha_A$. This parameter specifies how likely $A$ is to expand into a potentially new subtree; as $n_A$ and $n_\sigma$ grow this becomes increasingly unlikely.

We used the publically available adaptor grammar inference software described in Johnson et al. (2007), which we modified slightly as described below. The basic algorithm is a Metropolis-within-Gibbs or Hybrid MCMC sampler (Robert and Casella, 2004), which resamples the parse tree for each sentence in the training data conditioned on the parses for the other sentences. In order to produce sample parses efficiently the algorithm constructs a PCFG approximation to the adaptor grammar which contains one rule for each adapted subtree $\sigma$, and uses a Metropolis accept/reject step to correct for the difference between the true adaptor grammar distribution and the PCFG approximation. With the datasets described below less than $0.1\%$ of proposal parses from this PCFG approximation are rejected, so it is quite a good approximation to the adaptor grammar distribution.

On the other hand, at convergence this algorithm produces a sequence of samples from the posterior distribution over adaptor grammars, and this posterior distribution seems quite broad. For example, at convergence with the most stable of our models, each time a sentence's parse is resampled there is an approximately 25% chance of the parse changing. Perhaps this is not surprising given the comparatively small amount of training data and the fact that the models only use fairly crude distributional information.

As just described, adaptor grammars require the user to specify a concentration parameter $\alpha_A$ for each adapted nonterminal $A$. It's not obvious how this should be done. Previous work has treated $\alpha_A$ as an adjustable parameter, usually tying all of the $\alpha_A$ to some shared value which is adjusted to optimize task performance (say, word segmentation accuracy). Clearly, this is undesirable.

Teh et al. (2006) describes how to learn the concentration parameters $\boldsymbol{\alpha}$, and we modified their procedure for adaptor grammars. Specifically, we put a vague $\mathrm{Gamma}(10, 0.1)$ prior on each $\alpha_A$, and after each iteration through the training data we performed 100 Metropolis-Hastings resampling steps for each $\alpha_A$ from an increasingly narrow $\mathrm{Gamma}$ proposal distribution. We found that the performance of the models with automatically learned concentration parameters $\boldsymbol{\alpha}$ was generally as good as the models where $\boldsymbol{\alpha}$ was tuned by hand (although admittedly we only tried three or four different values for $\boldsymbol{\alpha}$).

## 3 Models of Sesotho word segmentation

We wanted to make our Sesotho corpus as similar as possible to one used in previous work on word segmentation. We extracted all of the non-child utterances from the LI–LV files from the Sesotho corpus of child speech (Demuth, 1992), and used the Sesotho gloss as our gold-standard corpus (we did not phonemicize them as Sesotho orthography is very close to phonemic). This produced 8,503 utterances containing 21,037 word tokens, 30,200 morpheme tokens and 100,113 phonemes. By comparison, the Brent corpus contains 9,790 utterances, 33,399 word tokens and 95,809 phonemes. Thus the Sesotho corpus contains approximately the same number of utterances and phonemes as the Brent corpus, but far fewer (and hence far longer) words. This is not surprising as the Sesotho corpus involves an older child and Sesotho, being an agglutinative language, tends to have morphologically complex words.

In the subsections that follow we describe a variety of adaptor grammar models for word segmentation. All of these models were given same Sesotho data, which consisted of the Sesotho gold-standard corpus described above with all word boundaries (spaces) and morpheme boundaries (hyphens) removed. We computed the f-score (geometric average of precision and recall) with which the models recovered the words or the morphemes annotated in the gold-standard corpus.

### 3.1 Unigram grammar

We begin by describing an adaptor grammar that simulates the unigram word segmentation model

| Model | word f-score | morpheme f-score |
|---|---|---|
| word | 0.431 | 0.352 |
| colloc | 0.478 | 0.387 |
| colloc2 | 0.467 | 0.389 |
| word − syll | 0.502 | 0.349 |
| colloc − syll | 0.476 | 0.372 |
| colloc2 − syll | 0.490 | 0.393 |
| word − morph | 0.529 | 0.321 |
| word − smorph | 0.556 | 0.378 |
| colloc − smorph | 0.537 | 0.352 |

Table 1: Summary of word and morpheme f-scores for the different models discussed in this paper.

proposed by Goldwater et al. (2006a). In this model each utterance is generated as a sequence of words, and each word is a sequence of phonemes. This grammar contains three kinds of rules, including rules that expand the nonterminal Phoneme to all of the phonemes seen in the training data.

$$\text{Sentence} \rightarrow \text{Word}^{+}$$
$$\underline{\text{Word}} \rightarrow \text{Phoneme}^{+}$$

Adapted non-terminals are indicated by underlining, so in the word grammar only the Word nonterminal is adapted. Our software doesn't permit regular expressions in rules, so we expand all Kleene stars in rules into right-recursive structures over new unadapted nonterminals. Figure 1 shows a sample parse tree generated by this grammar for the sentence:

u- e- nk- il- e kae
SM-OM-take-PERF-IN where
"You took it from where?"

This sentence shows a typical inflected verb, with a subject marker (glossed SM), an object marker (OM), perfect tense marker (PERF) and mood marker (IN). In order to keep the trees a managable size, we only display the root node, leaf nodes and nodes labeled with adapted nonterminals.

The word grammar has a word segmentation f-score of 43%, which is considerably below the 56% f-score the same grammar achieves on the Brent corpus. This difference presumably reflects the fact that Sesotho words are longer and more complex, and so segmentation is a harder task.

We actually ran the adaptor grammar sampler for

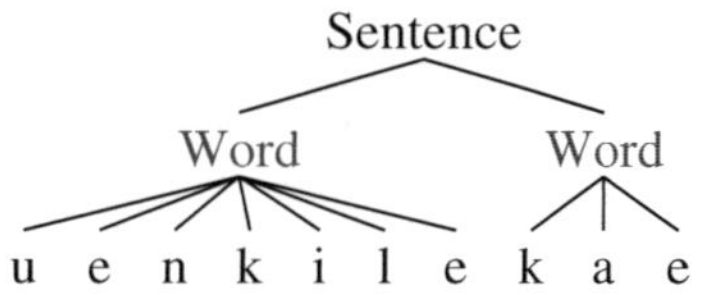


Figure 1: A sample (correct) parse tree generated by the word adaptor grammar for a Sesotho utterance.

the word grammar four times (as we did for all grammars discussed in this paper). Because the sampler is non-deterministic, each run produced a different series of sample segmentations. However, the average segmentation f-score seems to be very stable. The accuracies of the final sample of the four runs ranges between 42.8% and 43.7%. Similarly, one can compute the average f-score over the last 100 samples for each run; the average f-score ranges between 42.6% and 43.7%. Thus while there may be considerable uncertainty as to where the word boundaries are in any given sentence (which is reflected in fact that the word boundaries are very likely to change from sample to sample), the average accuracy of such boundaries seems very stable.

The final sample grammars contained the initial rules $R$, together with between 1,772 and 1,827 additional expansions for Word, corresponding to the cached subtrees for the adapted Word nonterminal.

### 3.2 Collocation grammar

Goldwater et al. (2006a) showed that incorporating a bigram model of word-to-word dependencies significantly improves word segmentation accuracy in English. While it is not possible to formulate such a bigram model as an adaptor grammar, Johnson (2008) showed that a similar improvement can be achieved in an adaptor grammar by explicitly modeling collocations or sequences of words. The colloc adaptor grammar is:

$$\begin{aligned} &\text{Sentence} \rightarrow \text{Colloc}^+ \\ &\underline{\text{Colloc}} \rightarrow \text{Word}^+ \\ &\underline{\text{Word}} \rightarrow \text{Phoneme}^+ \end{aligned}$$

This grammar generates a Sentence as a sequence of Colloc(ations), where each Colloc(ation) is a sequence of Words. Figure 2 shows a sample parse tree generated by the colloc grammar. In terms of word segmentation, this grammar performs much worse than the word grammar, with an f-score of 27%.

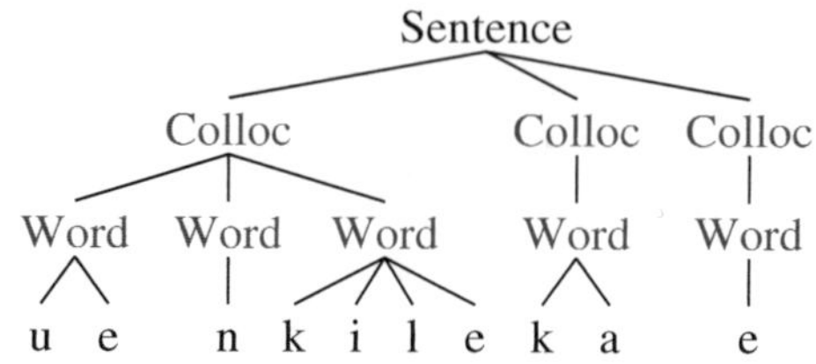


Figure 2: A sample parse tree generated by the colloc grammar. The substrings generated by Word in fact tend to be morphemes and Colloc tend to be words, which is how they are evaluated in Table 1.

In fact, it seems that the Word nonterminals typically expand to morphemes and the Colloc nonterminals typically expand to words. It makes sense that for a language like Sesotho, when given a grammar with a hierarchy of units, the learner would use the lower-level units as morphemes and the higher-level units as words. If we simply interpret the Word trees as morphemes and the Colloc trees as words we get a better word segmentation accuracy of 48% f-score.

### 3.3 Adding more levels

If two levels are better than one, perhaps three levels would be better than two? More specifically, perhaps adding another level of adaptation would permit the model to capture the kind of interword context dependencies that improved English word segmentation. Our colloc2 adaptor grammar includes the following rules:

$$\begin{aligned} &\text{Sentence} \rightarrow \text{Colloc}^+ \\ &\underline{\text{Colloc}} \rightarrow \text{Word}^+ \\ &\underline{\text{Word}} \rightarrow \text{Morph}^+ \\ &\underline{\text{Morph}} \rightarrow \text{Phoneme}^+ \end{aligned}$$

This grammar generates sequences of Words grouped together in collocations, as in the previous grammar, but each Word now consists of a sequence of Morph(emes). Figure 3 shows a sample parse tree generated by the colloc2 grammar.

Interestingly, word segmentation f-score is 46.7%, which is slightly lower than that obtained by the simpler colloc grammar. Informally, it seems that when given an extra level of structure the colloc2 model uses it to describe structure internal

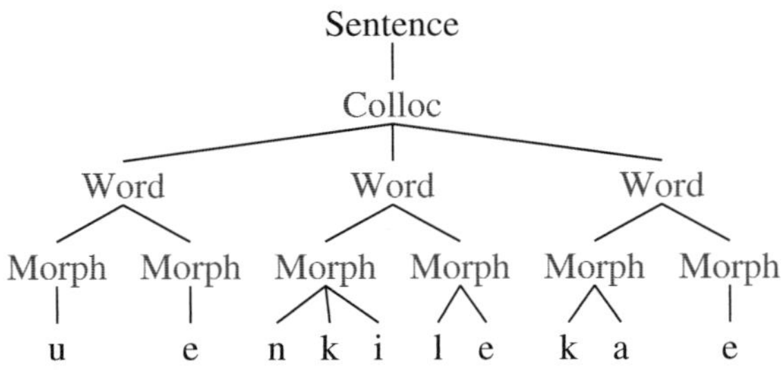


Figure 3: A sample parse tree generated by the colloc2 grammar.

to the word, rather than to capture interword dependencies. Perhaps this shouldn't be surprising, since Sesotho words in this corpus are considerably more complex than the English words in the Brent corpus.

## 4 Adding syllable structure

Johnson (2008) found a small but significant improvement in word segmentation accuracy by using an adaptor grammar that models English words as a sequence of syllables. The word – syll grammar builds in knowledge that syllables consist of an optional Onset, a Nuc(leus) and an optional Coda, and knows that Onsets and Codas are composes of consonants and that Nucleii are vocalic (and that syllabic consonsants are possible Nucleii), and learns the possible syllables of the language. The rules in the adaptor grammars that expand Word are changed to the following:

$$\underline{\text{Word}} \rightarrow \text{Syll}^+$$
$$\underline{\text{Syll}} \rightarrow (\text{Onset})\ \text{Nuc}\ (\text{Coda})$$
$$\underline{\text{Syll}} \rightarrow \text{SC}$$
$$\underline{\text{Onset}} \rightarrow \text{C}^+$$
$$\text{Nuc} \rightarrow \text{V}^+$$
$$\underline{\text{Coda}} \rightarrow \text{C}^+$$

In this grammar C expands to any consonant and V expands to any vowel, SC expands to the syllabic consonants '*l*', '*m*' '*n*' and '*r*', and parentheses indicate optionality. Figure 4 shows a sample parse tree produced by the word – syll adaptor grammar (i.e., where Words are generated by a unigram model), while Figure 5 shows a sample parse tree generated by the corresponding colloc – syll adaptor grammar (where Words are generated as a part of a Collocation).

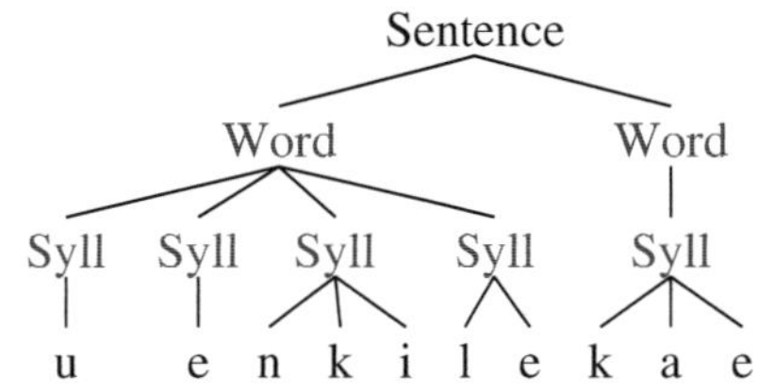


Figure 4: A sample parse tree generated by the word – syll grammar, in which Words consist of sequences of Syll(ables).

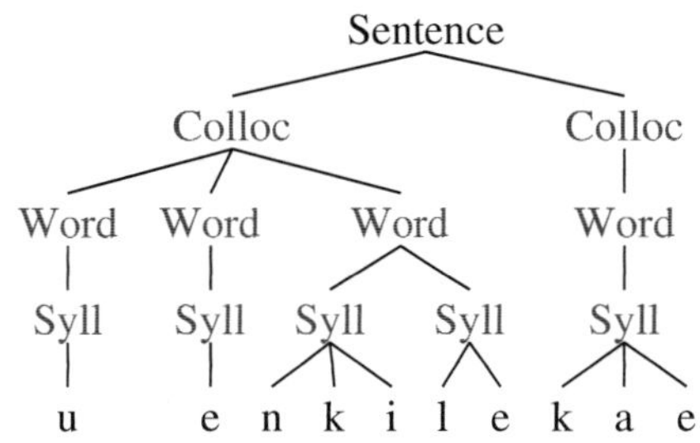


Figure 5: A sample parse tree generated by the colloc – syll grammar, in which Colloc(ations) consist of sequences of Words, which in turn consist of sequences of Syll(ables).

Building in this knowledge of syllable structure does improve word segmentation accuracy, but the best performance comes from the simplest word – syll grammar (with a word segmentation f-score of 50%).

### 4.1 Tracking morphological position

As we noted earlier, the various Colloc grammars wound up capturing a certain amount of morphological structure, even though they only implement a relatively simple unigram model of morpheme word order. Here we investigate whether we can improve word segmentation accuracy with more sophisticated models of morphological structure.

The word – morph grammar generates a word as a sequence of one to five morphemes. The relevant productions are the following:

$$\underline{\text{Word}} \rightarrow \text{T1}\ (\text{T2}\ (\text{T3}\ (\text{T4}\ (\text{T5}))))$$
$$\underline{\text{T1}} \rightarrow \text{Phoneme}^+$$
$$\underline{\text{T2}} \rightarrow \text{Phoneme}^+$$
$$\underline{\text{T3}} \rightarrow \text{Phoneme}^+$$
$$\underline{\text{T4}} \rightarrow \text{Phoneme}^+$$
$$\underline{\text{T5}} \rightarrow \text{Phoneme}^+$$

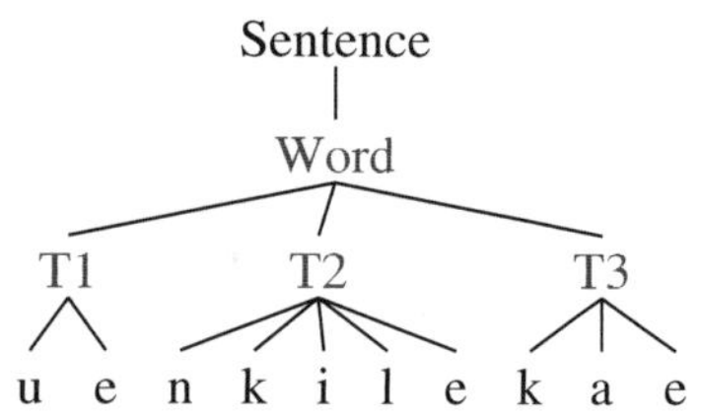


Figure 6: A sample parse tree generated by the word – morph grammar, in which Words consist of morphemes T1–T5, each of which is associated with specific lexical items.

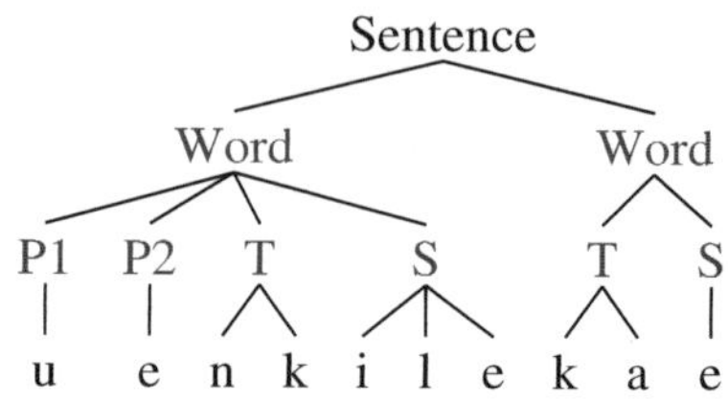


Figure 7: A sample parse tree generated by the word – smorph grammar, in which Words consist of up to five morphemes that satisfy prespecified ordering constraints.

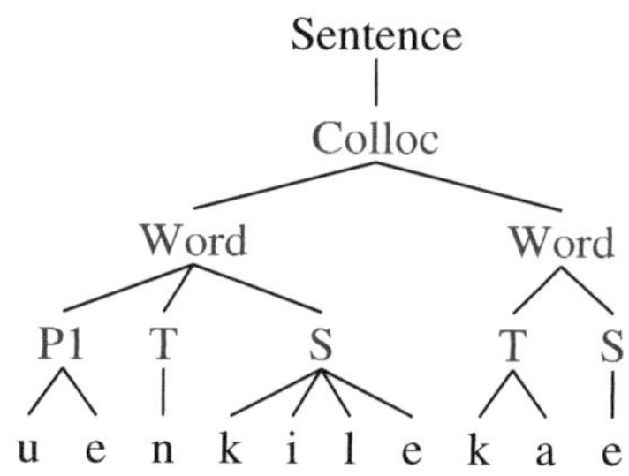


Figure 8: A sample parse tree generated by the colloc – smorph grammar, in which Colloc(ations) generate a sequence of Words, which in turn consist of up to five morphemes that satisfy prespecified ordering constraints.

While each morpheme is generated by a unigram character model, because each of these five morpheme positions is independently adapted, the grammar can learn which morphemes prefer to appear in which position. Figure 6 contains a sample parse generated by this grammar. Modifying the grammar in this way significantly improves word segmentation accuracy, achieving a word segmentation f-score of 53%.

Inspired by this, we decided to see what would happen if we built-in some specific knowledge of Sesotho morphology, namely that a word consists of a stem plus an optional suffix and zero to three optional prefixes. (This kind of information is often built into morphology learning models, either explicitly or implicitly via restrictions on the search procedure). The resulting grammar, which we call word – smorph, generates words as follows:

$$\underline{\text{Word}} \rightarrow (\text{P1}\,(\text{P2}\,(\text{P3})))\,\text{T}\,(\text{S})$$
$$\underline{\text{P1}} \rightarrow \text{Phoneme}^{+}$$
$$\underline{\text{P2}} \rightarrow \text{Phoneme}^{+}$$
$$\underline{\text{P3}} \rightarrow \text{Phoneme}^{+}$$
$$\underline{\text{T}} \rightarrow \text{Phoneme}^{+}$$
$$\underline{\text{S}} \rightarrow \text{Phoneme}^{+}$$

Figure 7 contains a sample parse tree generated by this grammar. Perhaps not surprisingly, with this modification the grammar achieves the highest word segmentation f-score of any of the models examined in this paper, namely 55.6%.

Of course, this morphological structure is perfectly compatible with models which posit higher-level structure than Words. We can replace the Word expansion in the colloc grammar with one just given; the resulting grammar is called colloc – smorph, and a sample parse tree is given in Figure 8. Interestingly, this grammar achieves a lower accuracy than either of the two word-based morphology grammars we considered above.

## 5 Conclusion

Perhaps the most important conclusion to be drawn from this paper is that the methods developed for unsupervised word segmentation for English also work for Sesotho, despite its having radically different morphological structures to English. Just as with English, more structured adaptor grammars can achieve better word-segmentation accuracies than simpler ones. While we find overall word segmentation accuracies lower than these models achieve on English, we also found some interesting differences in which factors contribute to better word segmentation. Perhaps surprisingly, we found little improvement to word segmentation accuracy when we modeled contextual dependencies, even though these are most important in English. But including either morphological structure or syllable structure in the model improved word segmentation accuracy markedly, with morphological structure making a larger impact. Given how important morphology is in Sesotho, perhaps this is no surprise after all.

## Acknowledgments

I'd like to thank Katherine Demuth for the Sesotho data and help with Sesotho morphology, my collaborators Sharon Goldwater and Tom Griffiths for their comments and suggestions about adaptor grammars, and the anonymous SIGMORPHON reviewers for their careful reading and insightful comments on the original abstract. This research was funded by NSF awards 0544127 and 0631667.

## References

N. Bernstein-Ratner. 1987. The phonology of parent-child speech. In K. Nelson and A. van Kleeck, editors, *Children's Language*, volume 6. Erlbaum, Hillsdale, NJ.

Christopher M. Bishop. 2006. *Pattern Recognition and Machine Learning*. Springer.

Rens Bod. 1998. *Beyond grammar: an experience-based theory of language*. CSLI Publications, Stanford, California.

M. Brent. 1999. An efficient, probabilistically sound algorithm for segmentation and word discovery. *Machine Learning*, 34:71–105.

Noam Chomsky. 1986. *Knowledge of Language: Its Nature, Origin and Use*. Praeger, New York.

Katherine Demuth. 1992. Acquisition of Sesotho. In Dan Slobin, editor, *The Cross-Linguistic Study of Language Acquisition*, volume 3, pages 557–638. Lawrence Erlbaum Associates, Hillsdale, N.J.

Sharon Goldwater, Thomas L. Griffiths, and Mark Johnson. 2006a. Contextual dependencies in unsupervised word segmentation. In *Proceedings of the 21st International Conference on Computational Linguistics and 44th Annual Meeting of the Association for Computational Linguistics*, pages 673–680, Sydney, Australia, July. Association for Computational Linguistics.

Sharon Goldwater, Tom Griffiths, and Mark Johnson. 2006b. Interpolating between types and tokens by estimating power-law generators. In Y. Weiss, B. Schölkopf, and J. Platt, editors, *Advances in Neural Information Processing Systems 18*, pages 459–466, Cambridge, MA. MIT Press.

Sharon Goldwater, Thomas L. Griffiths, and Mark Johnson. 2007. Distributional cues to word boundaries: Context is important. In David Bamman, Tatiana Magnitskaia, and Colleen Zaller, editors, *Proceedings of the 31st Annual Boston University Conference on Language Development*, pages 239–250, Somerville, MA. Cascadilla Press.

Sharon Goldwater. 2007. *Nonparametric Bayesian Models of Lexical Acquisition*. Ph.D. thesis, Brown University.

Yu Hu, Irina Matveeva, John Goldsmith, and Colin Sprague. 2005. Refining the SED heuristic for morpheme discovery: Another look at Swahili. In *Proceedings of the Workshop on Psychocomputational Models of Human Language Acquisition*, pages 28–35, Ann Arbor, Michigan, June. Association for Computational Linguistics.

Mark Johnson, Thomas L. Griffiths, and Sharon Goldwater. 2007. Adaptor Grammars: A framework for specifying compositional nonparametric Bayesian models. In B. Schölkopf, J. Platt, and T. Hoffman, editors, *Advances in Neural Information Processing Systems 19*, pages 641–648. MIT Press, Cambridge, MA.

Mark Johnson. 2008. Using adaptor grammars to identifying synergies in the unsupervised acquisition of linguistic structure. In *Proceedings of the 46th Annual Meeting of the Association of Computational Linguistics*, Columbus, Ohio, June. Association for Computational Linguistics.

Percy Liang, Slav Petrov, Michael Jordan, and Dan Klein. 2007. The infinite PCFG using hierarchical Dirichlet processes. In *Proceedings of the 2007 Joint Conference on Empirical Methods in Natural Language Processing and Computational Natural Language Learning (EMNLP-CoNLL)*, pages 688–697.

Rissanen. 1989. *Stochastic Complexity in Statistical Inquiry*. World Scientific Company, Singapore.

Christian P. Robert and George Casella. 2004. *Monte Carlo Statistical Methods*. Springer.

Y. W. Teh, M. Jordan, M. Beal, and D. Blei. 2006. Hierarchical Dirichlet processes. *Journal of the American Statistical Association*, 101:1566–1581.

# Invited Talk:
# Counting Rankings

**Jason Riggle**
University of Chicago
jriggle@uchicago.edu

## Abstract

In this talk, I present a recursive algorithm to calculate the *number* of rankings that are consistent with a set of data (optimal candidates) in the framework of Optimality Theory (OT; Prince and Smolensky 1993).[1] Computing this quantity, which I call $r$-volume, makes possible a simple and effective Bayesian heuristic in learning – *all else equal, choose candidates that are preferred by the highest number of rankings consistent with previous observations.* This heuristic yields an $r$-volume learning algorithm (RVL) that is guaranteed to make fewer than $k \lg k$ errors while learning rankings of $k$ constraints. This log-linear error bound is an improvement over the quadratic bound of Recursive Constraint Demotion (RCD; Tesar and Smolensky 1996) and it is within a logarithmic factor of the best possible mistake bound for any OT learning algorithm.

**Computing $r$-volume:** The violations in an OT tableau can be given as a $[n \times k]$ array of integers in which the first row $t_1$ corresponds to the winner. Following Prince (2002), the ranking information can be extracted by comparing $t_1$ with each 'losing' row $t_2, ..., t_n$ to create an Elementary Ranking Condition as follows: $erc(t_1, t_i) = \langle \alpha_1, ..., \alpha_k \rangle$ where $\alpha_j = \mathbf{L}$ if $t_{1,j} < t_{i,j}$, $\alpha_j = \mathbf{W}$ if $t_{1,j} > t_{i,j}$, and $\alpha_j = \boldsymbol{e}$ otherwise. The meaning of $\alpha$ is that at least one constraint associated with W dominates all those associated with L.

| *input* | $\mathbb{C}_1$ | $\mathbb{C}_2$ | $\mathbb{C}_3$ | | |
|---|---|---|---|---|---|
| *candidate* $t_1$ | * | ** | | *winner* | |
| *candidate* $t_2$ | ** | * | | $erc(t_1, t_2) = \langle \mathrm{W}, \mathrm{L}, e \rangle$ | i.e. $t_1$ beats $t_2$ if $\mathbb{C}_1$ outranks $\mathbb{C}_2$ |
| *candidate* $t_3$ | | | ** | $erc(t_1, t_3) = \langle \mathrm{L}, \mathrm{L}, \mathrm{W} \rangle$ | i.e. $t_1$ beats $t_3$ if $\mathbb{C}_3$ outranks $\mathbb{C}_1$ and $\mathbb{C}_2$ |
| *candidate* $t_4$ | | *** | * | $erc(t_1, t_4) = \langle \mathrm{L}, \mathrm{W}, \mathrm{W} \rangle$ | i.e. $t_1$ beats $t_4$ if $\mathbb{C}_2$ or $\mathbb{C}_3$ outranks $\mathbb{C}_1$ |

For a set $E$ of length-$k$ ERCs, $E - w_i$ denotes a set $E'$ derived from $E$ by removing ERCs with W in column $i$ and removing column $i$.

$$r\text{-vol}(E^k) = \sum_{1 \le i \le k} \begin{cases} 0 & \text{if } x_i = \mathrm{L} \text{ for } \textbf{any } x \in E \\ (k-1)! & \text{if } x_i = \mathrm{W} \text{ for } \textbf{all } x \in E \\ r(E - w_i) & \text{otherwise} \end{cases}$$

**Mistake bounds:** To make predictions, RVL selects in each tableau the candidate that yields the highest $r$-volume when the ERCs that allow it to win are combined with $E$ (the ERCs for past winners). To establish a mistake bound, assume that the RVL chooses candidate $e$ when, in fact, candidate $o$ was optimal according to the target ranking $\mathcal{R}_T$. Assuming $e \neq o$, the rankings that make $o$ optimal must be half or fewer of the rankings consistent with $E$ or else RVL would have chosen $o$. Because all rankings that make candidates other than $o$ optimal will be eliminated once the ERCs for $o$ are added to $E$, each error reduces the number of rankings consistent with all observed data by at least half and thus there can be no more than $\lg k!$ errors.

**Applications:** The $r$-volume seems to encode 'restrictiveness' in a way similar to Tesar and Prince's (1999) $r$-measure. As a factor in learning, it predicts typological frequency (cf. Bane and Riggle 2008) and priors other than the 'flat' distribution over rankings can easily be included to test models of ranking bias. More generally, this research suggests the concept of $g$-volume for any parameterized model of grammar.

[1]Full bibliography available on the Rutgers Optimality Archive (roa.rutgers.edu) with the paper Counting Rankings.



*Proceedings of the Tenth Meeting of the ACL Special Interest Group on Computational Morphology and Phonology*, page 28,
Columbus, Ohio, USA June 2008. 

# Three Correlates of the Typological Frequency of Quantity-Insensitive Stress Systems

**Max Bane** and **Jason Riggle**
Department of Linguistics
University of Chicago
Chicago, IL 60637, USA
bane@uchicago.edu, jriggle@uchicago.edu

## Abstract

We examine the typology of quantity-insensitive (QI) stress systems and ask to what extent an existing optimality theoretic model of QI stress can predict the observed typological frequencies of stress patterns. We find three significant correlates of pattern attestation and frequency: the trigram entropy of a pattern, the degree to which it is "confusable" with other patterns predicted by the model, and the number of constraint rankings that specify the pattern.

## 1 Introduction

A remarkable characteristic of human language is that the typological distribution of many linguistic properties is extremely uneven. For example, Maddieson's (1984) survey of phonemic inventories finds that a total of 921 distinct sounds are used by a sample of 451 languages, yet the average language employs only about 30 of those. Furthermore, some sounds are so commonly attested as to be almost universal (e.g., /m/, /k/), while others are vanishingly rare (/ʁ/, /œ/). Heinz (2007) combines two previous typologies of accentual stress (Bailey, 1995; Gordon, 2002), and finds that among a sample of 306 languages with quantity-insensitive (QI) stress systems, 26 distinct stress patterns are found,[1] while over 60% of the languages surveyed use one of just 3 of these patterns. If we begin to look at morphosyntactic or semantic properties, the combinatorics of possible systems veritably explodes, leaving each attested language with an even smaller slice of the logical possibilities.

Most typological studies have attempted to give accounts of linguistic phenomena that simultaneously:

- predict as many attested languages or patterns as possible, and
- predict as few unattested languages or patterns as possible.

We will refer to this goal as the "inclusion-exclusion" criterion of a linguistic model. Comparatively few attempts have been made to explain or predict the relative *frequencies* with which languages or patterns are observed to occur in cross-linguistic samples (though see Liljencrants and Lindblom 1972, de Boer 2000, Moreton to appear, and others for work proceeding in this direction).

This paper examines the typology of QI stress systems, as reported by Heinz (2007), and asks to what extent an existing optimality theoretic (Prince and Smolensky, 1993) model of QI stress, developed by Gordon (2002) to meet the inclusion-exclusion criterion, can predict the observed typological frequencies of stress patterns. Gordon's model predicts a total of 152 possible stress patterns, which, as far as we are aware, represent the current best attempt at satisfying the inclusion-exclusion criterion for QI stress, failing to generate only two attested stress patterns (unknown to Gordon at the time), and generating 128 unattested patterns. We show that Gordon's model can offer at least three novel, statistically significant predictors of which of the 152 generated patterns are actually attested, and of the

[1] These figures include only those quantity-insensitive stress patterns according to which there is exactly one possible assignment of stress per word length in syllables.



*Proceedings of the Tenth Meeting of the ACL Special Interest Group on Computational Morphology and Phonology*, pages 29–38,
Columbus, Ohio, USA June 2008. 

cross-linguistic frequencies of the attested patterns. Namely:

i. Of the 152 stress patterns predicted by Gordon's model, the attested and frequent ones exhibit significantly lower trigram entropy than the unattested and infrequent,

ii. the length of forms, in syllables, that must be observed to uniquely identify a stress pattern is significantly lower for the attested patterns than for the unattested, and

iii. the number of constraint rankings in Gordon's model that are consistent with a stress pattern is a significant predictor both of which patterns are attested and of the relative frequencies of the attested patterns.

In what follows, Section 2 presents an overview of the basic theoretical background and empirical facts of quantity-insensitive stress that guide this study, including a review of Heinz's (2007) typology and a description of Gordon's (2002) OT model. Section 3 then introduces the three proposed correlates of attestedness and frequency that can be applied to Gordon's framework, together with statistical analyses of their significance as predictors. Finally, Section 4 offers a discussion of the interpretation of these findings, as well as some concluding remarks.

## 2 Quantity-Insensitive Stress Patterns

### 2.1 Assumptions and Definitions

We will follow Gordon (2002) and Heinz (2007) in taking a stress system to be any accentual system that satisfies "culminativity" in the sense of Prince (1983); that is, any accentual system in which there is always one most prominent accentual unit per accentual domain. In this case, we assume that the accentual unit is the syllable, and that the domain is the prosodic word. Thus, any given syllable of a word may bear primary, secondary, or no stress (we ignore the possibility of tertiary or other stress), but there must always be exactly one primary stressed syllable per word.

We further restrict our attention in this study to quantity-insensitive (QI) stress systems, which are those stress systems according to which the assignment of stresses to a word's syllables depends only on the number of syllables present (a quantity assumed to be fixed when stress is assigned), and not on the segmental contents of the syllables. We will refer to "stress systems" and "stress patterns" interchangeably.

| $n$ | Albanian | Malakmalak |
|---|---|---|
| 2 | $\acute{\sigma}\sigma$ | $\acute{\sigma}\sigma$ |
| 3 | $\sigma\acute{\sigma}\sigma$ | $\sigma\acute{\sigma}\sigma$ |
| 4 | $\sigma\sigma\acute{\sigma}\sigma$ | $\acute{\sigma}\sigma\grave{\sigma}\sigma$ |
| 5 | $\sigma\sigma\sigma\acute{\sigma}\sigma$ | $\sigma\acute{\sigma}\sigma\grave{\sigma}\sigma$ |
| 6 | $\sigma\sigma\sigma\sigma\acute{\sigma}\sigma$ | $\acute{\sigma}\sigma\grave{\sigma}\sigma\grave{\sigma}\sigma$ |

Table 1: The stress assignments of $n$-syllable words for $2 \leq n \leq 6$ in the QI stress patterns of Albanian and Malakmalak.

As two concrete examples of QI stress systems, consider those of Albanian (Chafe, 1977; also shared by many other languages) and Malakmalak (an Australian language; Birk, 1976). These patterns are illustrated in Table 1 for words of length two through six syllables.[2] The former is a simple fixed system in which primary stress is always located on the penultimate syllable, while no other syllable bears stress. The latter is rather more complex, requiring stress on even numbered syllables from the right, the leftmost being primary. Crucially, neither system is sensitive to notions like syllabic weight, nor to any other properties of the syllables' contents.

Formally, one can consider a QI stress pattern up to length $n$ (in syllables), $P_n$, to be a set of strings over the alphabet $\Sigma = \{\sigma, \grave{\sigma}, \acute{\sigma}\}$:

(1) $P_n = \{w_2, \dots, w_n\}$,

where each $w_i$ encodes the locations of stress in a word of $i$ syllables, satisfying:

(2) $|w_i| = i, \quad w_i \in \Sigma^*$, and
$w_i$ contains $\acute{\sigma}$ exactly once.

Thus for a given maximum number of syllables $n$, there are

$$\prod_{i=2}^{n} i2^{(i-1)} = n! \cdot 2^{\frac{n(n-1)}{2}}$$

[2] Here and throughout this paper, $\sigma$ refers to an unstressed syllable, $\grave{\sigma}$ indicates a syllable bearing secondary stress, and $\acute{\sigma}$ indicates primary stress.

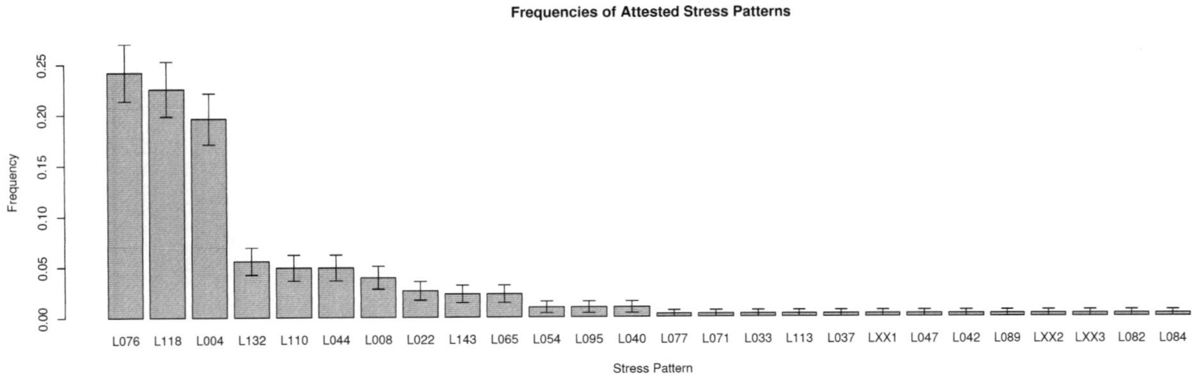


Figure 1: Frequency of attestation of each of the 26 distinct stress patterns. Error bars indicate standard Poisson sampling error.

logically possible QI stress patterns. We will follow Gordon (2002) by imposing a maximum word length of 8 syllables for purposes of distinguishing one stress pattern from another in the typology, and of determining the set of distinct patterns predicted by the model. We are therefore dealing with a universe of $8!2^{28}$ = 10,823,317,585,920 theoretically possible stress systems.

## 2.2 The Typology

The typological data on which this study is based are due to Heinz (2007), who has made them freely available.[3] This database is a combination of

- that from Bailey (1995), itself gathered from Halle and Vergnaud (1987) and Hayes (1995), and
- the collection put together by Gordon (2002) from previous surveys by Hyman (1977) and Hayes (1980), as well as from additional source grammars.

The combined database is intended to be fairly exhaustive, sampling a total of 422 genetically and geographically diverse languages with stress systems.

Of those 422 languages, 318 are identified as possessing quantity-insensitive stress, and we further confine our attention to the 306 of those with systems that uniquely determine the stress of each word as a function of syllable-count (i.e., with no optionality). We should note that it is possible for one language to contribute more than one distinct stress pattern to our dataset, as in the case of Lenakel (Lynch, 1974), for instance, which employs one regular pattern for nouns and another for verbs and adjectives.

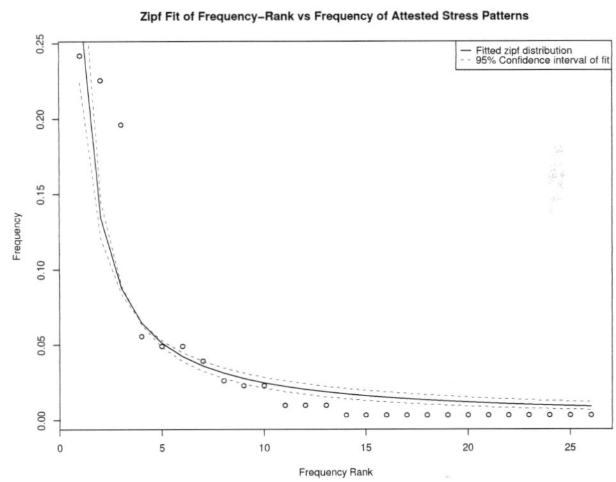


Figure 2: Regressed Zipf distribution of stress pattern frequencies; Zipf's exponent is found to be $1.05 \pm 0.15$ at $95\%$ confidence.

Between these 306 languages, we find a total of 26 distinct QI stress systems, which is quite a bit fewer than expected by chance, given the sample size and the 10.8 trillion *a priori* possible systems. Figure 1 shows the frequency with which each pattern is attested, arranged in decreasing order of frequency. The distribution of patterns is essentially Zipfian; a nonlinear regression of the frequencies against Zipf's law (using the Gauss-Newton method) achieves strong statistical significance ($p < 0.001$) and can account for 80.9% of the variance in

[3]The typology is available as a MySQL database at `http://www.ling.udel.edu/heinz/diss/`

| Constraint(s) | Penalizes... |
|---|---|
| ALIGNEDGE | each edge of the word with no stress. |
| ALIGN($\{\grave{\sigma}, \acute{\sigma}\}$, L/R) | each (primary or secondary) stressed syllable for each other (stressed or unstressed) syllable between it and the left/right edge. |
| ALIGN($\acute{\sigma}$, L/R) | each primary stressed syllable for each secondary stressed syllable between it and the left/right edge. |
| NONFINALITY | the last syllable if it is stressed. |
| *LAPSE | each adjacent pair of unstressed syllables. |
| *CLASH | each adjacent pair of stressed syllables. |
| *EXTLAPSE | each occurrence of three consecutive unstressed syllables. |
| *LAPSELEFT/RIGHT | the left/right-most syllable if more than one unstressed syllable separates it from the left/right edge. |
| *EXTLAPSERIGHT | the right-most syllable if more than two unstressed syllables separate it from the right edge. |

Table 2: Gordon's (2002) constraint set.

frequency (Figure 2).

The top three most common patterns, together accounting for over 60% of the sampled languages, are all simple fixed primary stress systems: fixed final stress (24.2% of systems), fixed initial stress (22.5% of systems), and fixed penultimate stress (19.6% of systems). It is possible that fixed primary systems may be somewhat overrepresented, as the descriptive sources can be expected to occasionally fail to report the presence of secondary stress; even so, the preponderance of such systems would seem to be substantial. The great majority of distinctly attested systems are quite rare, the median frequency being 0.65% of sampled languages. Some examples of cross-linguistically unlikely patterns include that of Georgian, with antepenultimate primary stress and initial secondary stress, and that of Içuã Tupi, which shows penultimate primary stress in words of four or fewer syllables, but antepenultimate stress in longer words.

There is some reason to believe that this sample is fairly representative of the whole population of QI stress patterns used by the world's languages. While it is true that the majority of sampled patterns are rare, it is by no means the case that the majority of sampled *languages* exhibit rare stress patterns. In fact, of the $N = 306$ sampled languages, just $n_1 = 13$ of them present stress patterns that are attested only once. Thus, according to the commonly used Good-Turing estimate (a distribution-free method of estimating type frequencies in a population from a sample of tokens; Good, 1953), we should expect to reserve approximately $\frac{n_1}{N} = 4.3\%$ of total probability-mass (or frequency-mass) for unseen stress patterns. In other words, we would be surprised to find that the actual population of languages contains much more than $\frac{N}{1-\frac{n_1}{N}} = 27.15$ distinct patterns, i.e., about one more than found in this sample.

### 2.3 Gordon's (2002) Model

Gordon (2002) has developed an optimality theoretic model of QI stress with the goal of satisfying the inclusion-exclusion criterion on an earlier subset of Heinz's (2007) typology. The model is footless, consisting of twelve constraints stated in terms of a metrical grid, without reference to feet or other metrical groupings (or, equivalently, simply in terms of linear $\{\sigma, \grave{\sigma}, \acute{\sigma}\}$-sequences). The twelve constraints are summarized in Table 2.

In addition to these, Gordon's model implements a sort of "meta-constraint" on rankings: he assumes that one of the primary alignment constraints ALIGN($\acute{\sigma}$, L/R) is always lowest ranked, so that in any given tableau either ALIGN($\acute{\sigma}$, L) or ALIGN($\acute{\sigma}$, R) is "active," but never both. Formally, we take this to mean that the model specifies two EVALS: an EVAL-L with ALIGN($\acute{\sigma}$, R) excluded from CON, and an EVAL-R with ALIGN($\acute{\sigma}$, L) excluded. The set of stress systems predicted by the whole model is then simply the union of the systems predicted by EVAL-L and by EVAL-R. This ranking restriction is meant to capture the probably universal generalization that primary stress always appears either to the left or right of the secondary stresses in a word, without vacillating from side to side for different word lengths. Gordon also assumes that candidate forms violating culminativity (i.e., forms without exactly one primary stressed syllable), are always excluded, either by some filter on the output of GEN or by an always highly ranked CULMINATE constraint against them.[4]

Gordon's model is capable of representing $2 \cdot 11! = 79{,}833{,}600$ QI stress grammars (11! rankings of the constraints associated with EVAL-L plus the 11! rankings for EVAL-R). We replicated Gordon's (2002) calculation of the factorial typology of distinct QI stress patterns that this grammar space predicts by implementing the constraints as finite-state transducers,[5] composing the appropriate combinations of these to produce finite-state implementations of EVAL-L and EVAL-R, respectively (see Riggle, 2004), and iteratively constructing consistent subsets of the members of the cross-products of candidate forms for each word length (two through eight syllables). See Riggle *et al* (2007) and Prince (2002) for the mathematical and algorithmic details.

The factorial typology of stress systems that is yielded agrees with that reported by Gordon (2002). The model predicts a total of 152 distinct possible systems. All but two of the 26 systems attested in Heinz's (2007) database are among these. The two patterns that Gordon's model fails to generate are those of Bhojpuri (as described by Tiwari, 1960; Shukla, 1981), and Içuã Tupi (Abrahamson, 1968). Both of these patterns were unknown to Gordon at the time he proposed his model, and each is attested only once in the typology.

In addition to failing to generate two of the attested stress systems, Gordon's model also predicts 128 patterns that are unattested. Gordon (2002) argues that a certain amount of overgeneration is to be expected of any model, since the majority of distinct attested systems are extremely rare; thus failure to observe a pattern in a limited sample is not strong evidence that the pattern is impossible. The Good-Turing estimate of unseen patterns (Section 2.2 above), however, suggests that significantly less overgeneration may still be desired. Gordon also argues that the overgenerated patterns are not pathologically different from the sorts of patterns that we do see (though Section 3 below describes several statistically detectable differences). In any case, Gordon's model of QI stress is among the most explicitly formulated approaches currently available, and offers a comparatively "tight" fit to the typological data.

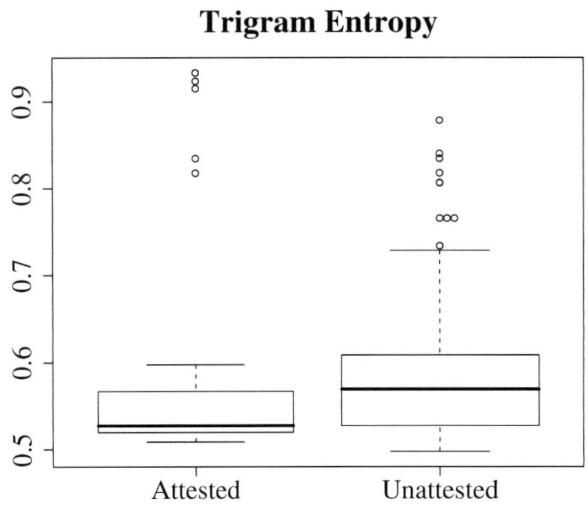


Figure 3: Trigram entropy (average bits per symbol) of attested versus unattested stress patterns; attested patterns have significantly lower entropy.

## 3 Predicting Typological Frequency

### 3.1 $k$-gram Entropy

A frequently offered and examined hypothesis is that, all else being equal, human communicative systems adhere to some principle of least effort (whether in terms of articulation or processing), preferring simple structures to complicated ones when additional complexity would afford no concomitant advantage in communicative efficiency or expressiveness. This line of reasoning suggests that typologically frequent properties should tend to exhibit

[4]We follow Gordon in remaining agnostic on this point, as the same set of possible stress patterns results from either implementation.

[5]The reader may notice that the ALIGN($\acute{\sigma}$, L/R) and ALIGN($\{\grave{\sigma}, \acute{\sigma}\}$, L/R) constraints (defined in Table 2) involve a kind of counting that cannot generally be accomplished by finite-state transducers. This is perhaps a theoretically undesirable property of Gordon's model (see Heinz *et al* (2005) for such a critique), but in any case, this general problem does not affect us here, as we ignore the possibility of words any longer than eight syllables (following Gordon; see Section 2.1).

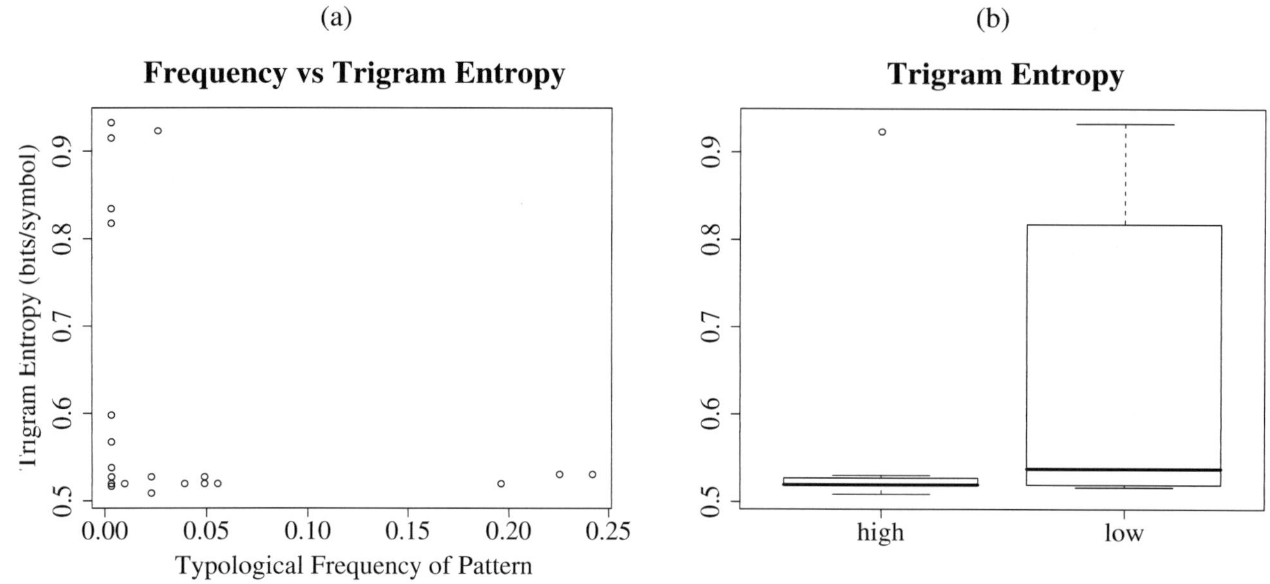


Figure 4: (a) typological frequency of attested stress patterns versus their trigram entropy, and (b) the trigram entropy of high-frequency (above median) patterns versus low-frequency (below median) patterns.

greater simplicity (according to some metric) than those that are rarer. One also expects, according to this hypothesis, that among the set of patterns predicted by a linguistic model such as Gordon's, the simpler ones should have a greater chance of attestation in typological samples. We find evidence consistent with both of these expectations in the case of QI stress systems, according to at least one information theoretic definition of complexity.

In order to calculate measures of complexity for each attested and predicted stress pattern, we construct bigram and trigram models of the transition probabilities between syllable types ($\sigma, \grave{\sigma}, \acute{\sigma}$) in forms of two through eight syllables for each pattern. That is, if each stress is taken to be a set of forms as in (1) (with $n = 8$ in this case), satisfying (2), then across all forms (i.e., word-lengths) one can count the number of occurrences of each $k$-length sequence ($k$-gram) of $\sigma, \grave{\sigma}, \acute{\sigma}$ and word boundaries to arrive at conditional probabilities for each syllable type (or a word boundary) given the previous $k-1$ syllables. With these probabilities one can then compute the Shannon entropy of the stress pattern as an index of its complexity; this is interpreted as the number of bits needed to describe the pattern (i.e., list its forms) under an efficient encoding, given the $k$-gram probability model. Stress patterns in which it is difficult to accurately predict the value of a syllable on the basis of the previous $k-1$ syllables will possess greater entropy, and thus be deemed more complex, than those in which such predictions can be made with greater accuracy.

We find that in the case of a bigram probability model ($k = 2$), the attested stress systems predicted by Gordon's model do not differ in entropy significantly[6] from those that are unattested; we also find no significant correlation between bigram entropy and the typological frequency of attested systems.

Under a trigram probability model ($k = 3$), however, entropy is a significant predictor of both whether a system is attested, and if it is attested, of its frequency in the sample. Figure 3 gives boxplots comparing the distribution of trigram entropy for those systems predicted by Gordon's model (plus the two unpredicted systems) that are attested versus those that are unattested. The attested QI stress systems are significantly less entropic than the unattested, according to a two-sided Mann-Whitney $U$-test: $U = 1196$, $p = 0.021$ (if the two unpredicted patterns are excluded, then $U = 923.5$, $p < 0.01$). Among attested systems, trigram entropy appears to bear a nonlinear relationship to typological fre-

[6]Throughout this study, we adopt a 95% confidence standard of significance, i.e., $p < 0.05$.

quency (see Figure 4). A significant linear correlation does not exist, and the 13 attested patterns with greater than median frequency have only mildly significantly lower entropy than the 13 with less than median frequency (according to another two-sided $U$-test: $U = 51.5$, $p = 0.0856$); if, however, the single high-frequency pattern with outlying entropy is excluded (the lone point indicated in Figure 4b), then the difference is more robustly significant: $U = 39.5$, $p = 0.0323$. Interestingly, the entropies of the above-median patterns are tightly constrained to a narrow band of values (variance 0.012 square bits/symbol), whereas the below-median patterns show much greater variation in their complexity (variance 0.028 square bits/symbol).

### 3.2 Confusability Vectors

The second metric we examine is motivated by considerations of learnability. Some QI stress patterns are very similar to each other in the sense that one must observe fairly long forms (i.e., forms with many syllables) in order to distinguish them from each other. For instance, in the case of Albanian and Malakmalak (Table 1 above), the two systems give identical stress assignments for words of two or three syllables; to tell them apart, one must compare words with four or more syllables. The degree of similarity, or "confusability" in this sense, between stress systems varies considerably for different pairs of languages. Assuming a tendency for short words to be encountered more frequently by language learners than long words, we might expect stress patterns that are easily identified at short word-lengths to be more faithfully acquired than those requiring longer observations for unambiguous identification. In particular, if we take the 152 patterns predicted by Gordon's model to constitute the set of possible QI stress systems, then we hypothesize that those patterns that stand out as unique at shorter lengths should be more typologically "stable": more likely to be attested, more frequently attested, or both.

To test this, we determine a *confusability vector* for each predicted pattern. This is simply a tuple of 7 integers in which the value of the $i$th component indicates how many of the other 151 predicted patterns the given pattern agrees with on forms of two through $i$+1 syllables. For example, the confusability vector of Albanian's (fixed penultimate primary; see Table 1) stress pattern is:

$$\langle 101, 39, 10, 0, 0, 0, 0 \rangle$$

This means that for words of two syllables, this stress system agrees with 101 of the other predicted systems, for words of two through three syllables it agrees with 39, and for two through four syllables it agrees with 10. Once words of five or more syllables are included in the comparison, it is unique among the stress patterns predicted, confusable with none.

A confusability vector allows us to calculate two quantities for a given stress pattern: its *confusability sum*, which is just the sum of all the components of the vector, and a *confusability pivot*, which is the number $i$ such that the $(i-1)$th component[7] of the vector is the first component with value 0. Thus the confusability sum of the fixed penultimate primary stress system is $101+39+10 = 150$, and its confusability pivot is 5, indicating that it achieves uniqueness among Gordon's predicted systems at five syllables.

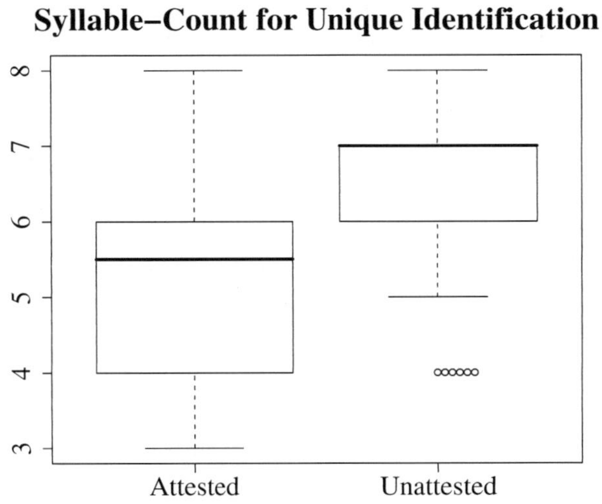


Figure 5: Attested stress patterns have significantly lower pivots than unattested ones.

We find that those of the predicted systems that are typologically attested have very significantly lower confusability pivots than the unattested systems (see Figure 5; Mann-Whitney $U$-test: $U = 1005.5$, $p < 0.001$). One might wonder whether this is simply due to the fact that primary-only stress

[7] We count vector components beginning at 1.

systems are most likely to be attested, and that such systems are independently expected to have lower confusability pivots than those with secondary stress (indeed, a two-sided Mann-Whitney test indicates that the pivots of primary-only systems are significantly lower: $U = 214$, $p < 0.01$). However, it appears that confusability pivots are in fact independently robust predictors of attestedness. When only the predicted patterns with secondary stress are considered, the pivots of the attested ones remain significantly lower than those of the unattested, albeit by a smaller margin ($U = 846$, $p = 0.027$). Confusability sums, on the other hand, are not significant predictors of attestedness in either case.

Neither pivots nor sums alone correlate well with the typological frequency of attested systems, but together they can predict approximately 27% of the variance in frequencies; a multilinear regression of the form

$$f(x) = \alpha + \beta s(x) + \gamma p(x),$$

where $f(x)$, $s(x)$, and $p(x)$ are the frequency, confusability sum, and pivot of pattern $x$, respectively, yields significant ($p < 0.05$) values for all coefficients ($R^2 = 0.271$).

### 3.3 Ranking Volume

The two typological predictors discussed above (entropy and confusability) are only weakly "post-theoretical" in the sense that, while they depend on a set of predicted stress patterns according to some linguistic theory or model (such as Gordon's), they can be computed without reference to the particular form of the model. In contrast, the third and last correlate that we consider is entirely specified and motivated by the optimality theoretic form of Gordon's model.

We define the *ranking volume*, or *$r$-volume*, of a language generated by an optimality theoretic model as the number of total constraint orderings (i.e., grammars) that specify the language. Riggle (2008) describes a method of applying the logic of Prince's (2002) elementary ranking conditions to compute this quantity. Using this method, we find that the number of rankings of Gordon's constraints that are consistent with a stress pattern predicted by his model is a significant correlate of attestedness,

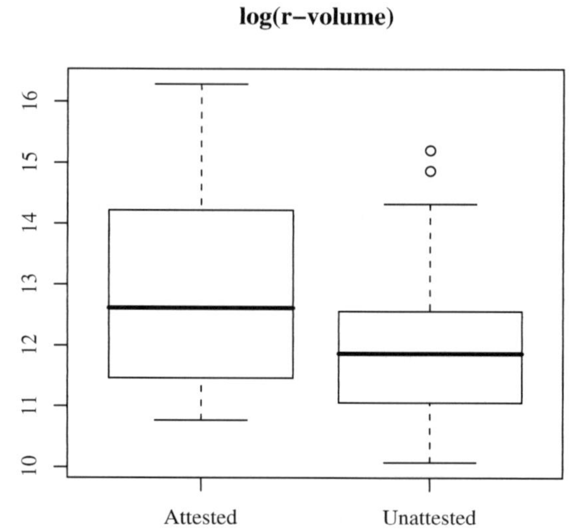


Figure 6: Of the predicted stress patterns, those that are attested are consistent with significantly more constraint-rankings. The natural logarithms of $r$-volume are shown here for greater ease of comparison.

and if the pattern is attested, of its typological frequency. In the case of Gordon's model, with its ranking meta-constraint and bifurcated EVAL (as described in Section 2.3), the total $r$-volume of each pattern is actually the sum of two quantities: the pattern's $r$-volume under the 11 constraints corresponding to EVAL-L (which excludes ALIGN($\acute{\sigma}$, R)), and its $r$-volume under the 11 constraints of EVAL-R (which conversely excludes ALIGN($\acute{\sigma}$, R)). Most of the predicted patterns are only generated by one of the EVALS, but some can be specified by either constraint set, and thus will tend to be consistent with more rankings. It just so happens that Gordon's choice of constraints ensures that these doubly generated patterns are of precisely the same sort that are typologically most frequent: fixed primary stress systems. This appears to account for much of the predictive power of $r$-volume in this model.

The distribution of $r$-volume among the 152 predicted stress patterns is almost perfectly Zipfian. A nonlinear Gauss-Newton regression of $r$-volumes against Zipf's law finds a highly significant fit (with Zipf's exponent $= 0.976 \pm 0.02$, $p < 0.001$) that accounts for 96.8% of the variance. The attested patterns tend to have significantly greater $r$-volumes than those unattested; two-sided Mann-Whitney's $U = 2113.5$, $p < 0.01$ (see Figure 6). On aver-

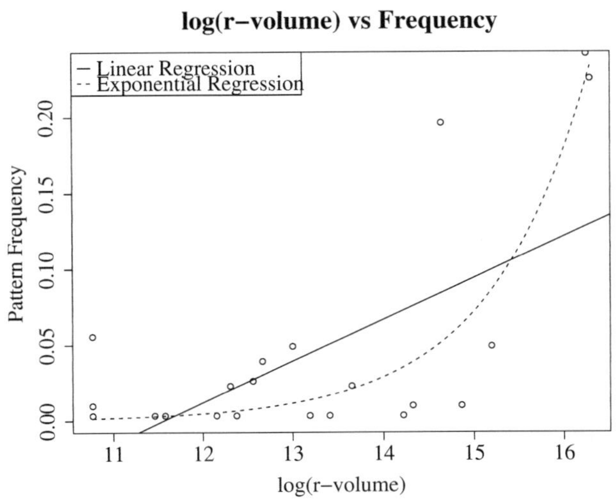


Figure 7: Linear and exponential regressions of typological frequency as a function of the natural logarithm of the pattern's $r$-volume.

age, the attested stress patterns are consistent with 1,586,437 rankings each, versus 299,118.1 rankings for the unattested ones.

Furthermore, the frequency of attested patterns has a strong linear correlation with $r$-volume: $R^2 = 0.7236$, $p < 0.001$. However, a linear relation is probably not appropriate, as a normal Q-Q plot of the residuals of the regression indicates an upper-quartile deviation from linearity, and Cook's distance metric indicates that several data-points exert disproportionate influence on the explained variance. Instead, typological frequency seems to be better modeled as a function of the logarithm of the $r$-volume; Figure 7 illustrates both a linear ($R^2 = 0.39$, $p < 0.05$) and exponential ($R^2 = 0.704$, $p < 0.001$) fit of frequencies to log-transformed $r$-volumes.

## 4 Interpretation and Future Work

The correlates of attestation and frequency reported here suggest novel ways that linguistic models might be used to make testable predictions about typology. Two of these correlates—$k$-gram entropy and confusability—are particularly general, their calculation requiring only the set of possible languages or patterns that a model can specify. It remains an interesting question whether these same quantities retain predictive power for other sorts of data and models than are considered here, and whether such correlations might fruitfully be incorporated into an evaluation metric for linguistic models.

The $r$-volume result motivates a particular line of further research on the nature of constraints in OT: how exactly the contents of a constraint set determine the distribution of $r$-volumes in the factorial typology. In addition, there are several other potentially relevant concepts in the literature, including Anttila's (1997, 2002, 2007) ranking-counting model of variation, Anttila and Andrus' (2006) "T-orders" and Prince and Tesar's (1999) "restrictiveness measure," whose relations to $r$-volume merit examination. Our results for $r$-volume in this case also suggest that a fully generalized notion of *parametric grammar volume* may be worth investigating across different kinds of models and various typological phenomena.

Insofar as the three correlates' strength as typological predictors depends on the set of stress patterns generated by Gordon's model, their significance is consistent with the hypothesis that the model is useful and has some predictive power. Such statistical significance is rather surprising, since Gordon's model was developed primarily as an attempt to satisfy the inclusion-exclusion criterion, without any explicit eye toward the kinds of predictions that these correlates seem to suggest it can make. This is especially true of $r$-volume, as it is the correlate most tightly coupled to the OT particulars of Gordon's model. These findings motivate further research on the general relationship, if any, between the inclusion-exclusion predictions of a model (optimality theoretic or otherwise) and its frequency predictions according to the measures presented here. On the other hand, the entropy and confusability results suggest the intriguing possibility of discarding such a model altogether, and instead picking the attested stress systems (and their frequencies) directly from the large pool of logically possible ones, according to these measures and others like them.

## Acknowledgements

We owe many thanks to Jeff Heinz for the typological data used in this study, and to Alan Yu, Morgan Sonderegger, and the anonymous reviewers of SIGMORPHON 2008 for insightful commentary.

## References


A. Abrahamson. 1968. Constrastive distribution of phoneme classes in Içuã Tupi. *Anthropological Linguistics*, 10(6):11–21.

Arto Anttila and Curtis Andrus. 2006. T-Orders. Manuscript, Stanford University.

Arto Anttila. 1997. Deriving variation from grammar. In Frans Hinskens, Roeland van Hout, and Leo Wetzels, editors, *Variation, Change and Phonological Theory*, pages 35–68. John Benjamins Press, Amsterdam/Philadelphia.

Arto Anttila. 2002. Variation and phonological theory. In Jack Chambers, Peter Trudgill, and Natalie Schilling-Estes, editors, *Handbook of Language Variation and Change*, pages 206–243. Blackwell, Malden, Mass.

Arto Anttila. 2007. Variation and optionality. In Paul de Lacy, editor, *The Cambridge Handbook of Phonology*. Cambridge University Press, Cambridge.

Todd Bailey. 1995. *Nonmetrical Constraints on Stress*. Ph.D. thesis, University of Minnesota.

D.B.W. Birk. 1976. *The Malakmalak Language, Daly River (Western Arnhem Land)*. Australian National University, Canberra.

Bart de Boer. 2000. Self-organization in vowel systems. *Journal of Phonetics*, 28:441–465.

I.J. Good. 1953. The population frequencies of species and the estimation of population parameters. *Biometrika*, 40(3/4):237–264, December.

Matthew Gordon. 2002. A factorial typology of quantity-insensitive stress. *Natural Language and Linguistic Theory*, 20(3):491–552.

Morris Halle and Jean-Roger Vergnaud. 1987. *An Essay on Stress*. MIT Press, Cambridge, MA.

Bruce Hayes. 1980. *A Metrical Theory of Stress Rules*. Ph.D. thesis, MIT, Cambridge, MA.

Bruce Hayes. 1995. *Metrical Stress Theory: Principles and Case Studies*. University of Chicago Press, Chicago.

Jeffrey Heinz, Greg Kobele, and Jason Riggle. 2005. Exploring the typology of quantity-insensitive stress systems without gradient constraints. Handout, 2005 Annual Meeting of the Linguistic Society of America.

Jeffrey Nicholas Heinz. 2007. *Inductive Learning of Phonotactic Patterns*. Ph.D. thesis, UCLA.

Larry Hyman. 1977. On the nature of linguistic stress. In Larry Hyman, editor, *Studies in Stress and Accent*, pages 37–82. University of Southern California, Department of Linguistics, Los Angeles.

Johan Liljencrants and Bjorn Lindblom. 1972. Numerical simulation of vowel quality systems: The role of perceptual contrast. *Language*, 48(4):839–862.

John Lynch. 1974. *Lenakel Phonology*. Ph.D. thesis, University of Hawaii.

Ian Maddieson. 1984. *Patterns of Sounds*. Cambridge University Press, Cambridge.

Elliott Moreton. in press. Learning bias as a factor in phonological typology. In Charles Chang and Anna Havnie, editors, *Proceedings of the 26th Meeting of the West Coast Conference on Formal Linguistics*.

Alan Prince and Paul Smolensky. 1993. Optimality theory: Constraint interaction in generative grammar. Ms., Rutgers University and University of Colorado, Boulder.

Alan Prince and Bruce Tesar. 1999. Learning phonotactic distributions. Ms., ROA 535.

Alan Prince. 1983. Relating to the grid. *Linguistic Inquiry*, 14:19–100.

Alan Prince. 2002. Entailed ranking arguments. *Rutgers Optimality Archive*, ROA-500.

Jason Riggle, Max Bane, James Kirby, and Jeremy O'Brien. 2007. Efficiently computing OT typologies. In *2007 Annual Meeting of the Linguistic Society of America*.

Jason Riggle. 2004. *Generation, Recognition, and Learning in Finite State Optimality Theory*. Ph.D. thesis, UCLA.

Jason Riggle. 2008. Counting rankings. Manuscript, University of Chicago. Draft available at `http://hum.uchicago.edu/~jriggle/`.

Shaligram Shukla. 1981. *Bhojpuri Grammar*. Georgetown University Press.

Udai Tiwari. 1960. *The Origin and Development of Bhojpuri*. Number 10 in Asiatic Society Monograph. Asiatic Society, Calcutta.

# Phonotactic Probability and the Māori Passive: A Computational Approach

**ʻŌiwi Parker Jones**
Oxford University Phonetics Laboratory
41 Wellington Square
Oxford, OX1 2JF, UK
oiwi.parkerjones@phon.ox.ac.uk

## Abstract

Two analyses of Māori passives and gerunds have been debated in the literature. Both assume that the thematic consonants in these forms are unpredictable. This paper reports on three computational experiments designed to test whether this assumption is sound. The results suggest that thematic consonants are predictable from the phonotactic probabilities of their active counterparts. This study has potential implications for allomorphy in other Polynesian languages. It also exemplifies the benefits of using computational methods in linguistic analyses.

| Active | Passive | Gloss |
|---|---|---|
| /ɸera/ | /ɸerahia/ | 'to spread' |
| /oma/ | /omakia/ | 'to run' |
| /inu/ | /inumia/ | 'to drink' |
| /eke/ | /ekeŋia/ | 'to climb' |
| /tupu/ | /tupuria/ | 'to grow' |
| /aɸi/ | /aɸitia/ | 'to embrace' |
| /huna/ | /hunaia/ | 'to conceal' |
| /kata/ | /kataina/ | 'to laugh' |
| /ako/ | /akona/ | 'to teach' |
| /heke/ | /hekea/ | 'to descend' |

Table 1: Examples of active and passive verbs in Māori.

## 1 Introduction

The Māori passive is perhaps the most famous problem in Polynesian linguistics. It has received attention from Williams (1971, first published in 1844), Biggs (1961), Hohepa (1967), Hale (1968; 1973; 1991), Kiparsky (1971), Kaye (1975), Kenstowicz and Kisseberth (1979), McCarthy (1981), Moorfield (1988), Sanders (1990; 1991), Harlow (1991; 2001; 2007), Bauer (1993), Blevins (1994), Kibre (1998), de Lacy (2004), and Boyce (2006). Some representative examples of active and passive verbs are given in Table 1 (Ryan, 1989).

Two types of analysis have been proposed for these data (Hale, 1968). These are known as the 'morphological' and 'phonological' analyses. For the subset of passives with thematic consonants, the analyses parse the data differently into stems and suffixes. To illustrate this, the examples from Table 1 have been parsed in Table 2 with hyphens inserted between the stems and suffixes. The thematic consonants have also been flagged.

In both types of analysis, the qualities of the thematic consonants are assumed to be unpredictable and are therefore lexicalized. To cite just one example, Blevins writes that "a consonant of *unpredictable* quality appears in the passive and gerundial forms, but this consonant is absent when the verb occurs unsuffixed" (Blevins, 1994, p. 29, my emphasis).

In the phonological analysis, the thematic consonants are lexicalized with the rest of the stem. The active forms are derived by a rule that deletes stem-final consonants. Although less obvious, the morphological analysis also lexicalizes the thematic consonants by allowing stems to be stored with 'diacritic features'. The reason for the diacritic features



*Proceedings of the Tenth Meeting of the ACL Special Interest Group on Computational Morphology and Phonology*, pages 39–48,
Columbus, Ohio, USA June 2008. 

| MOR | PHON | THEME |
|---|---|---|
| /ɸera-hia/ | /ɸerah-ia/ | /h/ |
| /oma-kia/ | /omak-ia/ | /k/ |
| /inu-mia/ | /inum-ia/ | /m/ |
| /eke-ŋia/ | /ekeŋ-ia/ | /ŋ/ |
| /tupu-ria/ | /tupur-ia/ | /r/ |
| /aɸi-tia/ | /aɸit-ia/ | /t/ |
| /huna-ia/ | /huna-ia/ | none |
| /kata-ina/ | /kata-ina/ | none |
| /ako-na/ | /ako-na/ | none |
| /heke-a/ | /heke-a/ | none |

Table 2: Morphological analyses (MOR), phonological analyses (PHON), and thematic consonants (THEME).

is to constrain the free combination of stems and suffixes, which, if unconstrained, would over-generate unattested passive forms. As an illustration, if we assume the exhaustive association of /inu/ with the diacritic feature [+m], then the stem would be allowed to combine with /-mia/, but not with any other suffixes. (In short, to store the diacritic feature is to lexicalize the quality of the thematic consonant.) Although lack of a diacritic feature is allowed for stems that take 'default' suffixes (/-tia/, /-ia/, or /-a/, depending on stem's size and composition), this would only be one thematic consonant (out of six) that would not be lexicalized; the phonological analysis could still be seen as lexicalizing the majority of the thematic consonants. Furthermore, a case could be made that the contrastive absence of a [+t] diacritic feature effectively lexicalizes /-tia/, too. Finally, it is worth noting that the purpose of the default suffixes is to provide analyses for previously unseen stems, such as nonce words or borrowings; in other words, the purpose of defaults is not to make /-tia/ non-lexical.

In this paper, I want to question the assumption that thematic consonants are unpredictable in Māori passives. To do so, I will focus on the phonotactic probabilities of active verbs as predictive of their passive and gerundial forms. I implemented the analysis as an artificial neural network, which I describe below. This follows from a rich tradition of using neural networks in phonology and morphology, as exemplified by the English past tense models of Rumelhart and McClelland (1987) and Plunkett and Marchman (1991). Incidentally, I chose neural networks to implement my analysis because of their computational properties, not because of an argument for the biological plausibility of my analysis. I suspect that similar results could have been obtained from another statistical formalism, like the $k$-nearest neighbor approach of TiMBL (Daelemans and van den Bosch, 2005).

The paper is laid out as follows. The network is described in section 2, the data and experimental methodology are presented in section 3, and the experimental results are reported in section 4. The discussion and conclusion follow in sections 5 and 6, respectively.

## 2 Network architecture and settings

The network I used in this study was designed to model a function from the representation of an active verb in Māori (alternatively, from a verb stem in the morphological analysis) to a set of output categories corresponding to passive formations (i.e., to a set of passive suffixes in the morphological analysis).

For the simulations in this study, I used a 3-layer feed-forward architecture with 199 input units, 100 hidden units, and 10 output units. The connectivity between adjacent layers was all-to-all. One fully activated bias unit was connected to every unit in the hidden and output layers (to model a thresholding effect and to aid learning). Figure 1 provides a rough blueprint of the network in 'slab' notation.

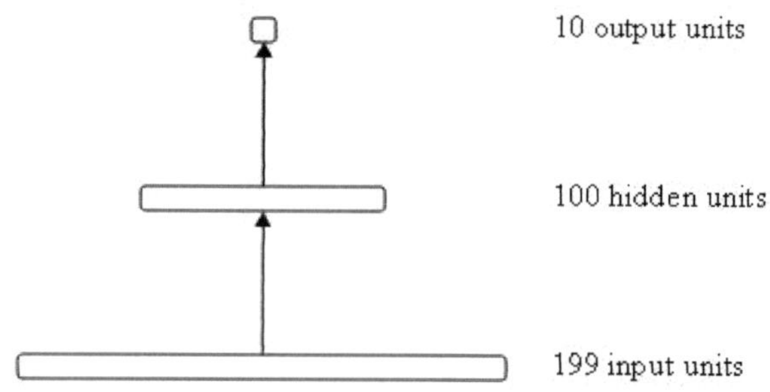


Figure 1: Network architecture; all-to-all connections between units in adjacent layers; bias unit not shown.

To calculate the output or activation of a node $i$ in

the network, I used a sigmoid function

$$a_i = \frac{1}{1 + e^{-net_i}}, \tag{1}$$

where $e$ is the exponential and $net_i$ is the net input to node $i$. As usual, the net input to node $i$ was defined as

$$net_i = \sum_j w_{ij} a_j, \tag{2}$$

where $w_{ij}$ refers to the weights on the connections from nodes $j$ to node $i$, and where $a_j$ refers to the activations of nodes $j$ (Plunkett and Elman, 1997). Learning was achieved using back-propagation and a learning rate of 0.1 (Werbos, 1974). No momentum was used. Let us turn now to the design of each layer in the network's architecture.

### 2.1 The input layer

There were 199 input units, where the number of input units was chosen to allow up to 18 segments in the input. Each segment was transformed into an 11-bit vector according to the feature encodings in Table 3. The unaccounted-for unit was used to tell the model if it was learning a passive or a gerund function; it can be thought of as specifying the semantic value PASS or NMLZ.

| | *vocalic* | *long* | *round* | *high* | *low* | *bilabial* | *alveolar* | *velar* | *plosive* | *fricative* | *nasal* |
|---|---|---|---|---|---|---|---|---|---|---|---|
| /a/ | 1 | 0 | 0 | 0 | 1 | 0 | 0 | 0 | 0 | 0 | 0 |
| /aː/ | 1 | 1 | 0 | 0 | 1 | 0 | 0 | 0 | 0 | 0 | 0 |
| /e/ | 1 | 0 | 0 | 0 | 0 | 0 | 0 | 0 | 0 | 0 | 0 |
| /eː/ | 1 | 1 | 0 | 0 | 0 | 0 | 0 | 0 | 0 | 0 | 0 |
| /i/ | 1 | 0 | 0 | 1 | 0 | 0 | 0 | 0 | 0 | 0 | 0 |
| /iː/ | 1 | 1 | 0 | 1 | 0 | 0 | 0 | 0 | 0 | 0 | 0 |
| /o/ | 1 | 0 | 1 | 0 | 0 | 0 | 0 | 0 | 0 | 0 | 0 |
| /oː/ | 1 | 1 | 1 | 0 | 0 | 0 | 0 | 0 | 0 | 0 | 0 |
| /u/ | 1 | 0 | 1 | 1 | 0 | 0 | 0 | 0 | 0 | 0 | 0 |
| /uː/ | 1 | 1 | 1 | 1 | 0 | 0 | 0 | 0 | 0 | 0 | 0 |
| /p/ | 0 | 0 | 0 | 0 | 0 | 1 | 0 | 0 | 1 | 0 | 0 |
| /t/ | 0 | 0 | 0 | 0 | 0 | 0 | 1 | 0 | 1 | 0 | 0 |
| /k/ | 0 | 0 | 0 | 0 | 0 | 0 | 0 | 1 | 1 | 0 | 0 |
| /ɸ/ | 0 | 0 | 0 | 0 | 0 | 1 | 0 | 0 | 0 | 1 | 0 |
| /h/ | 0 | 0 | 0 | 0 | 0 | 0 | 0 | 0 | 0 | 1 | 0 |
| /m/ | 0 | 0 | 0 | 0 | 0 | 1 | 0 | 0 | 0 | 0 | 1 |
| /n/ | 0 | 0 | 0 | 0 | 0 | 0 | 1 | 0 | 0 | 0 | 1 |
| /ŋ/ | 0 | 0 | 0 | 0 | 0 | 0 | 0 | 1 | 0 | 0 | 1 |
| /ɾ/ | 0 | 0 | 0 | 0 | 0 | 0 | 1 | 0 | 0 | 0 | 0 |
| /w/ | 0 | 0 | 0 | 0 | 0 | 1 | 0 | 0 | 0 | 0 | 0 |
| // | 0 | 0 | 0 | 0 | 0 | 0 | 0 | 0 | 0 | 0 | 0 |

Table 3: Māori phonemes and feature encodings.

I approached the representation of active verbs empirically. Three coding schemes were considered, one of which was segment-based and two of which were syllable-based. Table 4 provides a handful of examples in the segmental coding scheme. Notice that each representation is right-aligned within the matrix and that there are no gaps between the segments. Null phonemes were used to fill the empty cells so that each input vector would be exactly 199 bits long.

| | | 6 | 5 | 4 | 3 | 2 | 1 |
|---|---|---|---|---|---|---|---|
| /aː/ | ↦ | | | | | | aː |
| /uhi/ | ↦ | | | | u | h | i |
| /waiho/ | ↦ | | w | a | i | h | o |
| /inoi/ | ↦ | | | i | n | o | i |
| /tia/ | ↦ | | | | t | i | a |

Table 4: Examples of segmental coding.

For both syllabic coding schemes, I used a 3-cell sequence to represent a CVV syllable template. To illustrate this, the examples from Table 4 have been reanalyzed in Table 5 to be consistent with both syllabic coding schemes.

| | | Syll | | | Syll | | |
|---|---|---|---|---|---|---|---|
| | | C | V | V | C | V | V |
| /aː/ | ↦ | | | | | aː | |
| /uhi/ | ↦ | | u | | h | i | |
| /waiho/ | ↦ | w | a | i | h | o | |
| /inoi/ | ↦ | | i | | n | o | i |
| /tia/ | ↦ | t | i | | | a | |

Table 5: Examples of syllabic coding.

Within each syllable sequence (Syll) in Table 5, the first position (C) was reserved for an onset, the second position (V) was reserved for the primary vowel, and the third position (V) was reserved for the second vowel of a diphthong. Again, every representation was right-aligned. Any sequence of short vowels in an active verb was treated as a diphthong, unless the vowels were equal in quality or the second vowel was lower than the first. For example, /ei/ and /eo/ would be diphthongs, but /ee/ and /ea/ would be analyzed as hiatus.

The syllabic coding schemes differed in their treatment of a long vowel followed by a short vowel, where the two vowels had non-identical qualities and the second was not lower than the first (i.e., where they would be diphthongs if both were phonemically short). The first coding treated these sequences as diphthongs (Coding 1); the second did not (Coding 2). Table 6 contrasts the two syllabic schemes for the word /taːoɾo/ 'to break down'. Since de Lacy (2004) advanced the analysis on which I based Coding 2, I shall sometimes distinguish these schemes by referring to Coding 2 as 'the de Lacy analysis'.

| | Syll | | | Syll | | | Syll | | |
|---|---|---|---|---|---|---|---|---|---|
| | C | V | V | C | V | V | C | V | V |
| Coding 1 | | | | t | aː | o | ɾ | o | |
| Coding 2 | t | aː | | | o | | ɾ | o | |

Table 6: Two syllabic codings for /taːoɾo/.

In the section on experiments below, I report on which of these three schemes worked best. For now, my aim has been to motivate the network's input layer. Notice that 199 input units provides space for input representations of up to 6 syllables (6 syllables $\times$ 3 prosodic positions $\times$ 11 features $=$ 198), with room for the semantic unit mentioned above. None of the active verbs in the passive dataset required more than 6 syllables in any of the coding schemes.

### 2.2 The output layer

Since there were 10 passive categories in my dataset (corresponding to the passive suffixes in the morphological analysis, illustrated in Figure 2), 10 output units were employed in the network. It was considered appropriate to model membership to each category independently, as many verbs show multiple passive forms (as /motu/ 'to separate, wound' does in its passive forms /motu-hia/ and /motu-kia/). The key to reading the model's passive output can be given as the vector [/-hia/, /-kia/, /-mia/, /-ŋia/, /-ria/, /-tia/, /-ia/, /-ina/, /-na/, /-a/]. Although the model represents its outputs as bits, they can be interpreted by reference to this key. For example, the passive output for /tapa/ 'to name' should be [1, 0, 0, 0, 0, 0, 1, 1, 0, 0], since Ryan's dictionary attests /tapa-hia/, /tapa-ia/, and /tapa-ina/. Note that these alternative outputs are taken to represent 'free' variation within a single speaker, rather than dialectical variation between speakers.

While the main focus of the model is the Māori passive, the network can also be used to associate active verbs (alternatively, morphological verb stems) with their gerundial forms (i.e., gerund suffixes, in a morphological analysis). Although there are fewer gerund suffixes than passive suffixes, there is a well-known parallel between the existing gerund suffixes and the subset of passive suffixes with thematic consonants. Consider the vector [/-haŋa/, /-kaŋa/, /-maŋa/, /-ŋa/, /-ɾaŋa/, /-taŋa/, /-aŋa/, N/A, N/A, N/A], which can be used as the key for interpreting gerund outputs in the network. Notice that the passive and gerund keys both order the thematic consonants as in the vector [/h/, /k/, /m/, /ŋ/, /ɾ/, /t/, //, N/A, N/A, N/A]. (Here, the null segment // has parallels in both keys.) So, interpretation of the gerundial output can also be performed by lookup. For example, the target output for /ɸiːtiki/ 'to tie up' on the gerund task is [0, 0, 0, 0, 1, 0, 0, 0, 0, 0], since the dataset from Ryan's dictionary attests /ɸiːtiki-ɾaŋa/. Finally, output activations for the last three nodes are undefined in the gerund task. I would have interpreted a significant activation for any of them as a false prediction.

### 2.3 The hidden layer

In general, too few hidden units do not provide a network with enough computational power to learn a desired function; too many units will result in the network overfitting the data, in which case its ability to generalize will suffer. Given the dimensions of the input and output layers, I was able to estimate the required number of hidden units empirically. Starting with a conservatively small number of hidden units, I trained the network for 100 epochs on 371 patterns in the passive dataset (i.e., approximately 80% of 464 patterns, which did not contain any known loanwords), and then froze the network's weights and tested its predictions on 46 of the withheld patterns (i.e., approximately 10% of the passive dataset), measuring the mean squared error. I repeated this procedure for increasingly populated hidden layers, until a trend emerged suggesting an optimum number of hidden units to minimize the mean squared error on the test set. For this task, 100 hidden units seemed to work well. The results for the estimation of hidden units have been graphed in Figure 2.

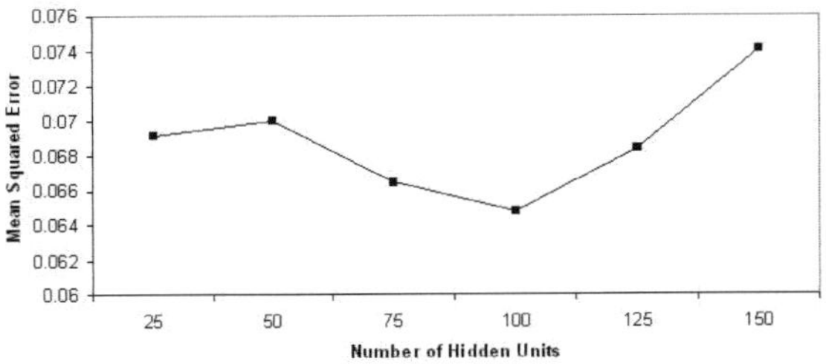


Figure 2: Minimizing error in the network.

## 3 Methodology

### 3.1 Data

The passive data in this study were drawn from the Māori-English section of *The Revised Dictionary of Modern Māori* (Ryan, 1989). This provided 476 passive patterns, 12 of which were flagged as English borrowings.

| Active | Passive | Gloss |
|---|---|---|
| /taraiwa/ | /taraiwa-tia/ | 'drive' |
| /raka/ | /raka-ina/ | 'lock' |
| /paera/ | /paera-tia/ | 'boil' |
| /wepu/ | /wepu-a/ | 'whip' |
| /perehi/ | /perehi-tia/ | 'press, print' |
| /paura/ | /paura-tia/ | 'powder' |
| /ɸaka-ho:nore/ | /ɸaka-ho:nore-tia/ | 'honor' |
| /pauna/ | /pauna-tia/ | 'to weigh' (< *pound*) |
| /parau/ | /parau-tia/ | 'plough' |
| /minita/ | /minita-tia/ | 'minister' |
| /ɸaka-rapihi/ | /ɸaka-rapihi-tia/ | 'to make rubbish of' |
| /parai/ | /parai-tia/ | 'fry' |

Table 7: 12 English borrowings with their passive forms.

Since I only found two gerund patterns in Ryan's dictionary (viz. /hu:pana-taŋa/ and /ɸi:tiki-raŋa/), I also searched the Māori Broadcast Corpus (MBC) for words ending as if they had gerundial suffixes (Boyce, 2006). This turned up 1537 gerund-like tokens, which reduced to 139 gerund-like types.

An overview of the data is provided in Tables 8 and 9. Table 8 shows that 464 passive patterns map to 28 output categories, the most populous of which contains 188 members. In other words, 188 verb stems take the passive suffix /-a/ and no other. By contrast, only one verb stem takes either /-tia/ or /-na/ as its passive suffixes. Similarly, Table 9 shows that 233 gerund-like patterns map to 16 output categories. For example, 120 (presumed) verb stems take the gerund suffix /-taŋa/.

| Category | Members | Category | Members |
|---|---|---|---|
| {/-a/} | 188 | {/-ŋia/, /-a/} | 2 |
| {/-tia/} | 112 | {/-ria/, /-tia/} | 2 |
| {/-hia/} | 33 | {/-hia/, /-ia/, /-ina/} | 1 |
| {/-na/} | 27 | {/-hia/, /-kia/} | 1 |
| {/-ŋia/} | 19 | {/-hia/, /-mia/} | 1 |
| {/-ia/} | 17 | {/-ia/, /-ina/, /-a/} | 1 |
| {/-ria/} | 16 | {/-ina/, /-a/} | 1 |
| {/-ina/} | 13 | {/-ŋia/, /-ia/} | 1 |
| {/-kia/} | 6 | {/-ŋia/, /-ria/} | 1 |
| {/-tia/, /-a/} | 6 | {/-ŋia/, /-tia/} | 1 |
| {/-mia/} | 4 | {/-ŋia/, /-tia/, /-a/} | 1 |
| {/-ia/, /-a/} | 3 | {/-ria/, /-ia/} | 1 |
| {/-hia/, /-a/} | 2 | {/-tia/, /-ina/} | 1 |
| {/-hia/, /-tia/} | 2 | {/-tia/, /-na/} | 1 |

Table 8: 464 passive patterns map to 28 output categories.

| Category | Members | Category | Members |
|---|---|---|---|
| {/-taŋa/} | 120 | {/-ŋa/, /-taŋa/} | 2 |
| {/-haŋa/} | 35 | {/-raŋa/, /-taŋa/} | 2 |
| {/-ŋa/} | 21 | {/-haŋa/, /-aŋa/} | 1 |
| {/-aŋa/} | 20 | {/-haŋa/, /-kaŋa/} | 1 |
| {/-raŋa/} | 16 | {/-haŋa/, /-maŋa/} | 1 |
| {/-kaŋa/} | 6 | {/-ŋa/, /-aŋa/} | 1 |
| {/-maŋa/} | 3 | {/-ŋa/, /-raŋa/} | 1 |
| {/-haŋa/, /-taŋa/} | 2 | {/-raŋa/, /-aŋa/} | 1 |

Table 9: 233 gerund-like patterns map to 16 categories.

### 3.2 Procedure

For the various experiments conducted, different subsets of the collected corpus were employed. In general, a sub-corpus was selected and then (randomly) split into training and testing sets. The size of these sets differed for the different experiments, since different amounts of relevant data were available. In every case, the stimuli consisted of input vectors and their corresponding target vectors.

Before training, the weights in the network were initialized using a random seed. Stimuli from the training set were then presented to the network randomly without replacement, so that each stimulus was seen once per epoch. Training lasted for 100 epochs. The weights were then frozen before each of the training stimuli were presented to the network again in order to validate the network's performance. The validated network was then presented with the test stimuli and its predictions were compared with the activations of the targets. In every experiment, the networks were run 5 times using 5 different random seeds to initialize the weights. I did this so that the results would be a little more robust. Performance was evaluated by taking the average percent correct over the 5 runs and variability was measured by calculating the standard deviation of the 5 runs.

Outputs were evaluated by fist rounding their activations to 0 or 1, before comparing them to the target patterns. It should be noted that this is a relatively liberal measure of the network's performance, given such alternatives as measuring the distance from output to target using a deviation $< 0.1$. Nonetheless, evaluation by rounding was justified on grounds that the only meaningful output patterns for the network were the non-negative integers 0 and 1.

I used chance as the null hypothesis when it was required for comparison with the network's performance, as chance represents the baseline for unpredictability. The chance of guessing the output activations correctly was calculated by assuming binary activations for the outputs (which is fair given the rounding of network outputs to 0 and 1). For 10 output nodes, $2^{10} = 1024$ possible guesses were possible. In such cases, the probability of guessing the correct output pattern for any stimulus was calculated as $\frac{1}{1024} \times 100 = 0.1\%$. Except where otherwise noted, the chance of guessing the right output patterns for $n$ stimuli was calculated as $\frac{n}{1024} \times 100$.

In some cases, I used other calculations as comparisons against the network's performance. I will introduce these where applicable.

## 4 Experimental results

### 4.1 Segmental and syllabic representations

As mentioned above, the question of input representation is an empirical one. I introduced three coding schemes in section 2.1 (a segmental one and two syllabic ones). In order to compare the schemes' ability to predict the passive forms (including the thematic consonants), a sub-corpus of 464 patterns was selected (i.e., the full set of 476 passives found in Ryan's dictionary minus the 12 loanwords). Since these stimuli had already been randomly split into 80%-10%-10% subsets to estimate the number of hidden units in the network, I started by reusing this split. The 10% used as a test set for the hidden units task were then lumped back into the training set, resulting in a random 90%-10% split (i.e., 418 training patterns and 46 test patterns). Each coding scheme was then applied to the same training and test sets, and the network was run as described in the methods section.

The results are summarized numerically in Table 10 and graphically in Figure 3. They suggest that either syllabic coding scheme is better than the segmental one, and that the de Lacy analysis is better than the alternative syllabic coding scheme (i.e., Coding 2 beats Coding 1). This suggests that it is better to represent a long vowel followed by a short vowel in Māori as two syllables.

| Coding Scheme | % Correct | Standard deviation |
|---|---|---|
| Segmental | 90.43 | 2.92 |
| Syllable 1 | 91.74 | 2.83 |
| Syllable 2 | 93.91 | 1.82 |

Table 10: Representation experiment results, rounded to the nearest hundredth.

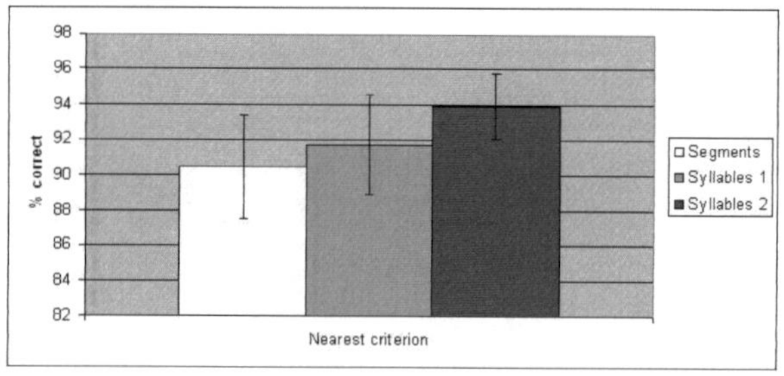


Figure 3: Test results for different representations of the stems, 5 runs apiece; error bars show standard deviations.

The results also challenge the assumption that thematic consonants are strongly unpredictable (i.e., governed by chance). I note that 30 of the test patterns did not take a suffix with a thematic consonant, while 15 did. So, of the 15 relevant test cases, the null hypothesis would have guessed 23.44% correct (i.e., $\frac{15}{2^6} \times 100$); I adjusted the calculation of the null hypothesis here to reflect the focus on just 6 of the 10 output patterns (i.e., the ones with thematic consonants). Without adjusting the calculation, the null hypothesis would have done much worse (cf. $\frac{15}{2^{10}} \times 100$). By contrast, the network predicts 46.67% correct (i.e., $\frac{7}{15} \times 100$), since it correctly predicted 7 out of the 15 patterns. So, the network correctly predicted 23.23% more of the thematic consonant patterns than chance. This suggests that lexicalization is not the only way to address thematic consonants in Māori. Since the problem can be specified in terms of active and passive verbs (rather than in terms of stems and suffixes), this also suggests that the Māori passive need not be framed in terms of the 'morphological' and 'phonological' analyses of Hale (1968).

The model also does well predicting the passive form of a verb in general. Note that the null hypothesis would only get 4.49% of the 46 test stimuli correct (i.e., $\frac{46}{1024} \times 100$). Using the de Lacy analysis, the network correctly predicted 93.91% of the 46 test stimuli, which is a massive difference of 89.42%. Moreover, the network also outperforms a 'majority choice' strategy, whereby all verb stems take the most frequent output category (i.e., {/-a/}). Majority choice correctly predicts 40.52% of the 464 passive patterns (i.e., $\frac{188}{464}$), which is 53.39% less than the network's coverage.

### 4.2 Gerunds

To test beyond the passive dataset, two sets of gerunds were considered. The idea was to see if training a network on a dataset of passives would be able to predict the suffix patterns of gerunds.

By training the network on the entire passive dataset 5 different times, and then testing each one on the 2 gerunds found in Ryan's dictionary, the network predicted the 100% of the results correct for all 5 runs. (For 2 test items, the null hypothesis would have only guessed $\frac{2}{1024} \times 100 = 0.2\%$ correct.)

Using the same training set, but testing the network on the 139 gerund-like words in the MBC, the network correctly predicted an average of 90.36% correct (with a standard deviation of 0.82). For 139 test patterns, the null hypothesis would only predict 13.57% correct. In both cases, the model does noticeably better than chance.

### 4.3 Loanwords

When new verbs enter the Māori language, speakers generalize their knowledge about the passive endings to them. How well does the network do at modeling this ability? 12 loanwords were flagged in the passive dataset. By training the network on the 464 non-loanword passives and then testing it on the 12 loanwords, the network got 100% correct for all 5 runs. Chance would only predict 1.17% of this test set correctly (i.e., $\frac{12}{1024} \times 100$).

The network also outperforms majority choice on this task, since majority choice for the 12 loanwords predicts 83.33% (i.e., $\frac{10}{12}$). (The most common output category for the 12 loanwords is {/-tia/}.)

In this case, however, there is probably a more charitable null hypothesis against which to compare the network's performance. I refer to the default analysis, where verbs take /-tia/, /-ia/, or /-a/. On this analysis, any stem containing more than two morae takes /-tia/ as its default, any stem containing fewer than three morae and ending with /a/ takes /-ia/ as its default, and any other stem (i.e., one containing fewer than three morae and not ending with /a/) takes /-a/. (Incidentally, one single-mora stem exists in my database; it is /ko/ 'to dig', which takes /-ia/.)

So, how does the default analysis compare with the network's analysis? Of the 12 loanwords in the passive database, the default analysis gets 91.67% correct (i.e., $\frac{11}{12}$). Again, the network gets 100% correct every time, for 5 runs. Interestingly, all but one of the 12 loanwords takes /-tia/, /-ia/, or /-a/. Furthermore, the exception, /ɾaka-ina/ (< English *lock*), would appear to be a systematic hole in the default analysis, since analogous examples exist, such as /tia-ina/ (< English *steer*) (Paul de Lacy, personal communication). Since both of these stems consist of fewer than three morae and end with /a/, the default analysis incorrectly predicts that their passive forms should be */ɾaka-ia/ and */tia-ia/, respectively. In other words, while the network only outperformed the default analysis by one example from the dataset, that one example would appear to be representative of a class of stems that the default analysis necessarily gets wrong, but which the neural network analysis could possibly get right. However, since the network needs to be run in order to see what it actually predicts, additional work would be needed to address this further.

## 5 Discussion

Thus far, the model has been evaluated on its performance. But while a model that performs well on a task is valuable in its own right, one would also like to understand how the model is succeeding. Neu-

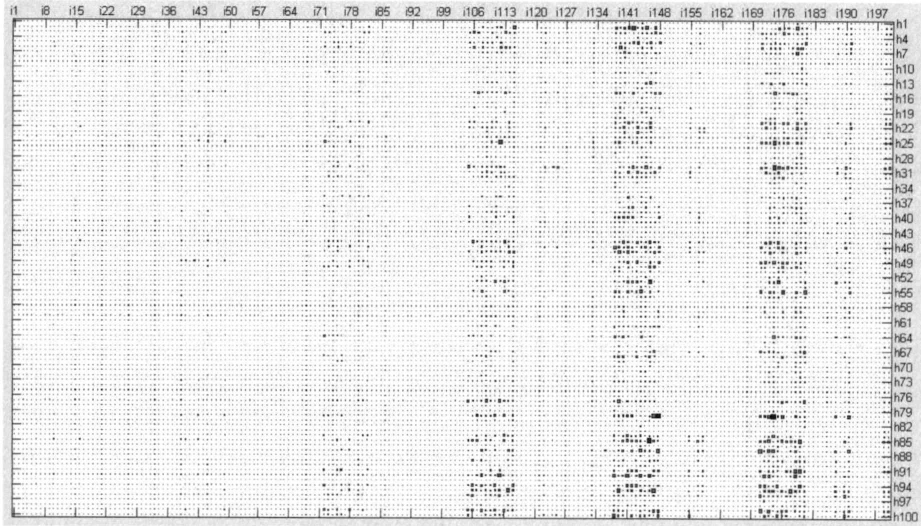


Figure 4: Hinton diagram for a typical weight matrix from input units (x-axis) to hidden units (y-axis).

ral network simulations are sometimes critiqued for being black box solutions, where a problem can be solved but the solution cannot be understood. Therefore, in this discussion section, I would like to begin to address the question of what properties in stem representations are responsible for the prediction of their output categories.

A few relevant sub-regularities have already been reported in the Māori literature, which are worth review. Citing Moorfield (1988, p. 66), Harlow reports that /-ina/ only occurs after words ending with /a/, while /-mia/ only occurs after words ending with /o/ and /u/ (i.e., the [$+round$] vowels); his examples, with the stem-final vowels underlined, are /hua̲-ina/ 'be named', /aroha̲-ina/ 'be loved', /ɸaka-ŋaro̲-mia/ 'be made to disappear', and /inu̲-mia/ 'be drunk' (Harlow, 2007, p. 117). Although these observations provide necessary but not sufficient conditions for inferring a passive suffix from a verb stem, they exemplify the type of pattern that one might like to find. The problem is to find better patterns in the verb stems.

For ideas of what to investigate, we might look inside one of the trained networks. Figure 4 illustrates the weights from input units to hidden units in a network trained on the Māori passive data using the de Lacy coding scheme (from section 4.1). Notice the dark vertical bands around inputs 176, 141, and 113 (there are fainter bands around input 78 and 43, and faint and narrow bands around input 190 and 155). These bands represent stronger weights (both positive and negative) between the two layers in the network. In order to understand the network's performance, we might ask what these bands represent. Given that the syllabic coding scheme organizes the segments into vowels and consonants in a similar pattern, one hypothesis would be that the vertical bands represent vowels in the input; a complementary hypothesis would hold that they represent consonants in the input. While this is a rather crude distinction to make, it begins to narrow down the hypothesis space.

To test such hypotheses, we may use 'degraded' inputs. For example, to test one hypothesis, one might replace all consonants in the input representations with null phonemes; to test the other hypothesis, one might replace all vowels in the input representations with null phonemes. An example of these degraded input representations is given in Table 11 for the word /ɸera/ 'to spread'.

In a preliminary study (running the network just once), I found that the model with vowel-only input outperformed the model with consonant-only input by a slight margin. Further investigation is surely needed. But the methodological use of degraded inputs provides a way to probe which parts of these representations contribute most to the model's performance.

Additional studies might use degraded inputs with only the final syllables represented compared with

| | Syll | | | Syll | | |
|---|---|---|---|---|---|---|
| | C | V | V | C | V | V |
| All segments | ϕ | e | | ɾ | a | |
| No consonants | | e | | | a | |
| No vowels | ϕ | | | ɾ | | |

Table 11: Three representations of /ϕera/ 'to spread'. The top one is an uncorrupted input using the de Lacy syllabic coding. The bottom two are degraded in different ways: one has no consonants, the other has no vowels.

ones in which only the penultimate or antipenultimate syllables are represented; they might even narrow down which phonetic features predict which passive and gerundial categories.

## 6 Conclusion

The work described here is clearly preliminary with respect to the problem of predicting passives and gerunds in Māori. But the experimental results are suggestive, especially as they challenge the long-held assumption that thematic consonants cannot be predicted. This research has implications for future investigations of allomorphy in Māori and other Polynesian languages, since Polynesian allomorphy has never before been explored using phonotactic probabilities (at least to the best of my knowledge).

In general, a computational approach makes it much easier to run complex statistical analyses over large datasets (compared with manual analyses using paper and pen). The success of utilizing statistics in this study exemplify the benefits of using computational methods in linguistics.


## Acknowledgments

For various feedback, I am grateful to acknowledge John Coleman, Julien Mayor, Sharon Goldwater, Paul de Lacy, Doug Ball, Mary Boyce, and three anonymous reviewers. This research was supported by a Lamakū Scholarship. All imperfections are my own.


## References


Winifred A. Bauer. 1993. *Maori*. Routledge, London and New York.

Bruce Biggs. 1961. The structure of New Zealand Maaori. *Anthropological Linguistics*, 3:1–53.

Juliette Blevins. 1994. A phonological and morphological reanalysis of the Maori passive. *Te Reo*, 37:29–53.

Mary Teresa Boyce. 2006. *A Corpus of Modern Spoken Māori*. Ph.D. thesis, Victoria University of Wellington.

Walter Daelemans and Antal van den Bosch. 2005. *Memory-Based Language Processing*. Cambridge University Press, Cambridge.

Paul de Lacy. 2004. Maximal words and the Maori passive. In John McCarthy, editor, *Optimality Theory in Phonology: A Reader*, pages 495–512. Blackwell, Oxford.

Kenneth Hale. 1968. Review of Hohepa (1967). *Journal of the Polynesian Society*, 77:83–99.

Kenneth Hale. 1973. Deep-surface canonical disparities in relation to analysis and change: An Australian example. In Thomas Sebeok, editor, *Current Trends in Linguistics 11*, pages 401–458. The Hague, Mouton.

Kenneth Hale. 1991. Remarks on G. Sanders' "Levelling in the history of Polynesian passive formations. *Journal of the Polynesian Society*, 100:99–101.

Ray Harlow. 1991. Consonant dissimilation in Maori. In *Currents in Pacific Linguistics: Papers in Austronesian Languages and Ethnolinguistics in honour of George W. Grace*, pages 117–128. Australian National Universiy, Canberra.

Ray Harlow. 2001. *A Māori Reference Grammar*. Pearson Education, Auckland.

Ray Harlow. 2007. *Māori: A Linguistic Introduction*. Cambridge University Press, Cambridge.

Patrick W. Hohepa. 1967. *A Profile Generative Grammar of Maori*. Indiana University Press, Bloomington, Indiana.

J. Kaye. 1975. A functional explanation for rule ordering in phonology. In R. Grossman, L.J. San, and T. Vance, editors, *Papers from the Parasession on Functionalism*. Chicago Linguistics Society, Chicago.

Michael Kenstowicz and Charles Kisseberth. 1979. *Generative Phonology: Description and Theory*. Academic Press, San Diego.

Nicholas Kibre. 1998. Formal property inheritance and consonant/zero alternations in Maori verbs. Rutgers Optimality Archive 285.

Paul Kiparsky. 1971. Historical linguistics. In William Dingwall, editor, *A Survey of Linguistic Science*, pages 577–649. University of Maryland Press, College Park, Maryland.

John J. McCarthy. 1981. The role of the evaluation metric in the acquisition of morphology. In C.L. Baker and John J. McCarthy, editors, *The Logical Problem of Language Acquisition*, pages 218–248. MIT Press, Cambridge, Massachusetts.

John C. Moorfield. 1988. *Whanake I Te Kākano*. Longman Paul, Auckland.

Kim Plunkett and Jeffrey L. Elman. 1997. *Exercises in Rethinking Innateness: A Handbook for Connectionist Simulations*. MIT Press, Cambridge, Massachusetts.

Kim Plunkett and Virginia Marchman. 1991. U-shaped learning and frequency effects in a multi-layered perceptron: Implications for child language acquisition. *Cognition*, 38:43–102.

David E. Rumelhart and James L. McClelland. 1987. Learning the past tenses of English verbs: Implicit rules or parallel distributed processing. In Brian MacWhinney, editor, *Mechanisms of Language Acquisition*, pages 194–248. Erlbaum, Mahwah, New Jersey.

P.M. Ryan. 1989. *The Revised Dictionary of Modern Māori*. Heinemann Education, Auckland, third edition.

Gerald Sanders. 1990. On the analysis and implications of Maori verb alternations. *Lingua*, 80:149–196.

G. Sanders. 1991. Levelling and reanalysis in the history of Polynesian passive formations. *Journal of the Polynesian Society*, 100:71–91.

Paul J. Werbos. 1974. *Beyond Regression: New Tools for Prediction and Analysis in the Behavioral Sciences*. Ph.D. thesis, Harvard University.

H.W. Williams. 1971. *A Dictionary of the Maori Language*. Government Printer, Wellington, seventh edition. Originally published in 1844.

# Evaluating an Agglutinative Segmentation Model for ParaMor

**Christian Monson, Alon Lavie, Jaime Carbonell, Lori Levin**
Language Technologies Institute
Carnegie Mellon University
Pittsburgh, PA 15217, USA
{cmonson, alavie, jgc, lsl}@cs.cmu.edu

## Abstract

This paper describes and evaluates a modification to the segmentation model used in the unsupervised morphology induction system, ParaMor. Our improved segmentation model permits multiple morpheme boundaries in a single word. To prepare ParaMor to effectively apply the new agglutinative segmentation model, two heuristics improve ParaMor's precision. These precision-enhancing heuristics are adaptations of those used in other unsupervised morphology induction systems, including work by Hafer and Weiss (1974) and Goldsmith (2006). By reformulating the segmentation model used in ParaMor, we significantly improve ParaMor's performance in all language tracks and in both the linguistic evaluation as well as in the task based information retrieval (IR) evaluation of the peer operated competition Morpho Challenge 2007. ParaMor's improved morpheme recall in the linguistic evaluations of German, Finnish, and Turkish is higher than that of any system which competed in the Challenge. In the three languages of the IR evaluation, our enhanced ParaMor significantly outperforms, at average precision over newswire queries, a morphologically naïve baseline; scoring just behind the leading system from Morpho Challenge 2007 in English and ahead of the first place system in German.

## 1 Unsupervised Morphology Induction

Analyzing the morphological structure of words can benefit natural language processing (NLP) applications from grapheme-to-phoneme conversion (Demberg et al., 2007) to machine translation (Goldwater and McClosky, 2005). But many of the world's languages currently lack morphological analysis systems. Unsupervised induction could facilitate, for these lesser-resourced languages, the quick development of morphological systems from raw text corpora. Unsupervised morphology induction has been shown to help NLP tasks including speech recognition (Creutz, 2006) and information retrieval (Kurimo et al., 2007b). In this paper we work with languages like Spanish, German, and Turkish for which morphological analysis systems already exist.

The baseline ParaMor algorithm which we extend here competed in the English and German tracks of Morpho Challenge 2007 (Monson et al., 2007b). The peer operated competitions of the Morpho Challenge series standardize the evaluation of unsupervised morphology induction algorithms (Kurimo et al., 2007a; 2007b). The ParaMor algorithm showed promise in the 2007 Challenge, placing first in the linguistic evaluation of German. Developed after the close of Morpho Challenge 2007, our improvements to the ParaMor algorithm could not officially compete in this Challenge. However, the Morpho Challenge 2007 Organizing Committee (Kurimo et al., 2008) graciously oversaw the quantitative evaluation of our agglutinative version of ParaMor.

### 1.1 Related Work

A variety of approaches to unsupervised morphology induction have shown promise in past work: Here we highlight three techniques which have been used in a number of unsupervised morphology induction algorithms. Since character sequences are less predictable at morpheme boundaries than within any particular morpheme (see discussion in section 2.1), a first unsupervised mor-



*Proceedings of the Tenth Meeting of the ACL Special Interest Group on Computational Morphology and Phonology*, pages 49–58,
Columbus, Ohio, USA June 2008. 

phology induction technique measures the predictability of word-internal character sequences. Harris (1955) was the first to propose the branching factor of the character tree of a corpus vocabulary as a measure of character predictability. Character trees have been incorporated into a number of more recently proposed unsupervised morphology induction systems (Schone and Jurafsky, 2001; Wicentowski, 2002; Goldsmith, 2006; Bordag, 2007). Johnson and Martin (2003) generalize from character trees and model morphological character sequences with minimized finite state automata. Bernhard (2007) measures character predictability by directly computing transitional probabilities between substrings of words.

A second successful technique has used the minimum description length principle to capture the morpheme as a recurrent structure of morphology. The Linguistica system of Goldsmith (2006), the Morfessor system of Creutz (2006), and the system described in Brent et al. (1995) take this approach.

A third technique leverages inflectional paradigms as the organizational structure of morphology. The ParaMor algorithm, which this paper extends, joins Snover (2002), Zeman (2007), and Goldsmith's Linguistica in building morphology models around the paradigm.

ParaMor tackles three challenges that face morphology induction systems which Goldsmith's Linguistica algorithm does not yet address. First, section 2.2 of this paper introduces an agglutinative segmentation model. This agglutinative model segments words into as many morphemes as the data justify. Although Goldsmith (2001) and Goldsmith and Hu (2004) discuss ideas for segmenting individual words into more than two morphemes, the implemented Linguistica algorithm, as presented in Goldsmith (2006), permits at most a single morpheme boundary in each word. Second, ParaMor decouples the task of paradigm identification from that of word segmentation (Monson et al., 2007b). In contrast, morphology models in Linguistica inherently encode both a belief about paradigm structure on individual words as well as a segmentation of those words. Without ParaMor's decoupling of paradigm structure from specific segmentation models, our algorithm for agglutinative segmentation (section 2.2) would not have been possible. Third, the evaluation of ParaMor in this paper is over much larger corpora than any published evaluation of Linguistica. Goldsmith (2006) segments the Brown corpus of English, which, after discarding numbers and punctuation, has a vocabulary size of 47,607 types. Using Linguistica, Creutz (2006) successfully segments a Finnish corpus of 250,000 tokens (approximately 130,000 types), but Creutz notes that Linguistica is memory intensive and not runable for larger corpora. In the evaluations of Morpho Challenge 2007, ParaMor segmented the words from corpora with over 42 million tokens and vocabularies as large as 2.2 million types.

## 2 ParaMor

This section briefly outlines the high level structure of ParaMor as described in detail in Monson et al. (2007a; 2007b). ParaMor takes the inflectional paradigm as the basic building block of morphology. A paradigm is a mutually substitutable set of morphological operations. For example, most adjectives in Spanish inflect for two paradigms. First, adjectives are marked for *gender*: an *a* suffix marks *feminine*, an *o masculine*. Then Spanish adjectives mark *number*: an *s* suffix signals *plural*, while no marking, *Ø* in this paper, indicates *singular*. The four surface forms of the cross-product of the *gender* and *number* paradigms on the Spanish word for 'beautiful' are then: *bello*, *bella*, *bellos*, and *bellas*.

ParaMor is a two stage algorithm. In the first stage, ParaMor identifies candidate paradigms which likely model suffixes of morphological paradigms and their cross-products. Since some 70% of the world's languages are significantly suffixing (Dryer, 2005), ParaMor only attempts to identify suffix paradigms. ParaMor's first stage consists of three pipelined steps. In the first step, ParaMor searches a space of candidate partial paradigms, called schemes, for those which possibly model suffixes of true paradigms. The second step merges selected schemes which appear to model the same paradigm. And in the third step, ParaMor discards scheme clusters which likely do not model true paradigms.

The second stage of the ParaMor algorithm segments word forms using the candidate paradigms identified in the first stage. Section 2.2 of this paper introduces a new segmentation model for ParaMor's second stage that allows more than one morpheme boundary in a single word—as is

| Rank | Model of: Noun | Model of: Adjective | Verb: ar | Verb: er | Verb: ir | Derivation | Good | Error: Stem Internal | Error: Suffix Internal | Error: Chance | | Candidate Suffixes | | Candidate Stems |
|---|---|---|---|---|---|---|---|---|---|---|---|---|---|---|
| 1 | • | • | | | | | • | | | | 2 | Ø.s | 5513 | apoyada, barata, hombro, oficina, reo, ... |
| 2 | | • | | | | | • | | | | 4 | a.as.o.os | 899 | apoyad, captad, dirigid, junt, próxim, ... |
| 3 | | | • | | | | | | • | | 14 | Ø.ba.ban.da.das.do.dos.n.ndo.r.ron.rse.rá.rán | 25 | apoya, disputa, lanza, lleva, toma, ... |
| 5 | | | • | | | | • | | | | 15 | a.aba.aban.ada.adas.ado.ados.an.ando.ar.aron.arse.ará.arán.ó | 24 | apoy, desarroll, disput, lanz, llev, ... |
| 11 | | • | | | | • | | • | | | 5 | ta.tamente.tas.to.tos | 22 | cier, direc, insóli, modes, sangrien, ... |
| 12 | | | • | | | • | | | • | | 14 | Ø.ba.ción.da.das.do.dos.n.ndo.r.ron.rá.rán.ría | 16 | acepta, concentra, fija, provoca, ... |
| 13 | | | • | | | | • | | | | 15 | a.aba.ada.adas.ado.ados.an.ando.ar.aron.ará.arán.e.en.ó | 20 | apoy, declar, enfrent, llev, tom, ... |
| 30 | | | | • | • | | • | | | | 11 | a.e.en.ida.idas.ido.idos.iendo.ieron.ió.ía | 15 | cumpl, escond, recib, transmit, vend, ... |
| 1000 | | | | | | | | | | • | 3 | Ø.g.gs | 4 | h, k, on, s |
| 1566 | | | | | • | | • | | | | 4 | ido.idos.ir.iré | 6 | conclu, cumpl, distribu, exclu, reun, segu |
| 2000 | | | | | | • | | • | | | 2 | lia.liana | 5 | austra, ita, ju, sici, zu |
| 3000 | | | | | | | | | | • | 3 | Ø.a.anar | 4 | all, am, g, s |
| 4000 | | | | | | | | | | • | 3 | Ø.e.ince | 4 | l, pr, qu, v |
| 8000 | | | • | | | | | • | | | 2 | trada.tramos | 3 | concen, demos, encon |

Table 1. Candidate partial paradigms, or schemes, that the baseline ParaMor algorithm selected during its first step, search, of its first stage, paradigm identification. This baseline ParaMor run was over a Spanish newswire corpus of 50,000 types. While some selected schemes contain suffixes from true paradigms, other schemes contain incorrectly segmented candidate suffixes.

needed to correctly segment Spanish *plural* adjectives. As this agglutinative segmentation model relies on the paradigms learned in ParaMor's first stage, section 2.1 presents solutions to two types of paradigm model error that the baseline ParaMor system makes. The solutions to these two error types are similar in nature to ideas proposed in the unsupervised morphology induction work of Hafer and Weiss (1974) and Goldsmith (2006).

## 2.1 Precision at Paradigm Identification

Table 1 presents 14 of the more than 8000 schemes identified during one baseline run of ParaMor's scheme search step. Each row of Table 1 lists a scheme that was selected while searching over a Spanish newswire corpus of 50,000 types. On the far left of Table 1, the *Rank* column states the ordinal rank at which that row's scheme was selected during the search procedure: the first scheme ParaMor selects is *Ø.s*; *a.as.o.os* is the second; *ido.idos.ir.iré* is the 1566$^{th}$ selected scheme, etc. The right four columns of Table 1, present raw data on the selected schemes, giving the number of candidate suffixes in that scheme, the proposed suffixes themselves, the number of candidate stems in the scheme, and a sample of those candidate stems. Each candidate stem in a ParaMor scheme forms a word that occured in the input corpus with each candidate suffix belonging to that scheme; for example, from the first selected scheme, the candidate stem *apoyada* joins to the candidate suffix *s* to form the word *apoyadas* 'supported *(adjective feminine plural)*'—a word which occured in the Spanish newswire corpus.

Between the rank on the left and the scheme details on the right of Table 1, are columns which categorize the scheme on its success, or failure, to model a true paradigm of Spanish. A dot appears in the columns marked *Noun*, *Adjective*, or *Verb* if the majority of the candidate suffixes in a row's scheme attempt to model suffixes in a paradigm of that part of speech. A dot appears in the *Derivation* column if one or more candidate suffixes of the scheme models a Spanish derivational suffix. The *Good* column is marked if the candidate suffixes of a scheme take the surface form of true paradigmatic suffixes. Initially selected schemes in Table 1 that correctly capture suffixes of real Spanish paradigms are the 1$^{st}$, 2$^{nd}$, 5$^{th}$, 13$^{th}$, 30$^{th}$, and 1566$^{th}$ selected schemes. While some smaller paradigms of Spanish are perfectly identified (including *Ø.s*, which marks singular and plural on many nouns and adjectives, and the adjectival cross-product paradigm of gender and number, *a.as.o.os*) many selected schemes do not satisfactorily model Spanish suffixes. Incorrect schemes in Table 1 are marked in the *Error* columns.

The vast majority of unsatisfactory paradigm models fail for one of two reasons. First, many schemes contain candidate suffixes which systematically misanalyze word forms. These schemes consistently hypothesize either stem-internal or suffix-internal morpheme boundaries. Schemes which hypothesize incorrect morpheme boundaries include the 3rd, 11th, 12th, 2000th, and 8000th selected schemes of Table 1. Among these, the 3rd and 12th selected schemes place morpheme boundaries internal to true suffixes. For example, the 3rd selected scheme contains truncated forms of suffixes that occur correctly in the 5th selected scheme. Symmetrically, the candidate suffixes in the 11th, 2000th, and 8000th selected schemes hypothesize morpheme boundaries internal to true Spanish stems, inadvertently including portions of stems within their suffix lists. In a random sample of 100 schemes from the 8240 schemes that the baseline ParaMor algorithm selects over our Spanish corpus, 59 schemes hypothesized an incorrect morpheme boundary.

The second most prevalent reason for model failure occurs when the candidate suffixes of a scheme are related not by belonging to the same paradigm, but rather by a chance co-occurrence on a few candidate stems of the text. Schemes which arise from chance string collisions in Table 1 include the 1000th, 3000th, and 4000th selected schemes. The string lengths of the candidate stems and candidate suffixes of these chance schemes are often quite short. The longest candidate stem in any of the three chance-error schemes of Table 1 is three characters long; and all three selected schemes propose the suffix Ø, which has length zero. Short stems and short suffixes in selected schemes are easily explained combinatorially: The inventory of possible strings grows exponentially with the length of the string. Because there just aren't very many length one, length two, or even length three strings, it should come as no surprise when a variety of candidate suffixes happen to occur attached to the same set of short stems. In our random sample of 100 initially selected schemes, 35 were erroneously selected as a result of a chance collision of word types.

The next two sub-sections present solutions to the two types of paradigm model failure in the baseline algorithm that are exemplified in Table 1. These first two extensions aim to improve precision by reducing the number of schemes ParaMor erroneously selects.

### Correcting Morpheme Boundary Errors

Most of the baseline selected schemes which incorrectly hypothesize a morpheme boundary do so at stem-internal positions. Indeed, in our random sample of 100 schemes, 51 of the 59 schemes with morpheme boundary errors incorrectly hypothesized a boundary stem-internally. For this reason, the baseline ParaMor algorithm already discarded schemes that likely misplace a boundary stem-internally (Monson et al., 2007b). Although there are fewer schemes that misplace a morpheme boundary suffix-internally, suffix-internal error schemes contain short suffixes that can generalize to segment a large number of word forms. (See section 2.2 for a description of ParaMor's morphological segmentation model). To measure the influence of suffix-internal error schemes on morpheme segmentation, we examined ParaMor's baseline segmentations of a random sample of 100 word forms from the 50,000 words of our Spanish corpus. In these 100 words, 82 morpheme boundaries were introduced that should not have been. And 40 of these 82 incorrectly proposed boundaries were placed by schemes which hypothesized a morpheme boundary internal to true suffixes.

To address the problem of suffix-internal misplaced boundaries we adapt an idea originally proposed by Harris (1955) and extended by Hafer and Weiss (1974): Take any string $t$. Let $F$ be the set of strings such that for each $f \in F$, $t.f$ is a word form of a particular natural language. Harris noted that when the boundaries between $t$ and each $f$ fall at morpheme boundaries, the strings in $F$ typically begin in a wide variety of characters; but when the $t$-$f$ boundaries are morpheme-internal, each legitimate word final string must first complete the erroneously split morpheme, and so the strings in $F$ will begin with one of a very few characters. This argument similarly holds when the roles of $t$ and $f$ are reversed. Hafer and Weiss (1974) describe a number of variations to Harris' letter variety algorithm. Their most successful variation uses entropy to measure character variety.

Goldsmith's (2006) Linguistica algorithm pioneered the use of entropy in a paradigm-based unsupervised morphology induction system. Linguistica measures the entropy of stem-final characters in a set of initially selected paradigm models. When entropy falls below a threshold, Linguistica considers relocating the morpheme boundary of each word covered by that paradigm model. If, after boundary relocation, the resulting description length of Linguistica's morphology model decreases, Linguistica accepts the relocated boundaries.

To identify suffix-internal morpheme boundary errors among ParaMor's initially selected schemes, we follow Hafer and Weiss (1974) and Goldsmith (2006) in using entropy as a measure of the variety in boundary-adjacent character distributions. In a ParaMor style scheme, the candidate stems form a set of word-initial strings, and the candidate suffixes a set of word-final strings. If a scheme's stems end in a very few unique characters, the scheme has likely hypothesized an incorrect suffix-internal morpheme boundary. Consider the 3rd selected scheme in Table 1. All 25 of the 3rd scheme's stems end in the character 'a'. Consequently, we measure the entropy of the distribution of final characters in each scheme's candidate stems. Where Linguistica modifies paradigm models which appear to incorrectly place morpheme boundaries, our extension to ParaMor permanently removes schemes. To avoid introducing a free parameter, our extension to ParaMor flags a scheme as a likely boundary error only when virtually all of that scheme's candidate stems end in the same character. We flag a scheme if its entropy is below a threshold set close to zero, 0.5. The baseline ParaMor algorithm discards schemes which it believes hypothesize an incorrect stem-internal morpheme boundary only after the scheme clustering step of ParaMor's paradigm identification stage. Our extension follows suit: If we flag more than half of the schemes in a cluster as likely proposing a suffix-internal boundary, then we discard that cluster. Referencing Table 1, this first extension to ParaMor successfully removes both the 3rd and the 12th selected schemes.

#### Correcting Chance String Collision Errors

Scheme errors due to chance string collisions are the second most prevalent error type. As described above, the string lengths of the candidate stems and suffixes of chance schemes are typically short. When the stems and suffixes of a scheme are short, then the underlying types which support a scheme are also short. Where the baseline ParaMor algorithm explicitly builds schemes over all types in a corpus, we modify ParaMor to exclude short types from the vocabulary during morphology induction. Goldsmith (2006) also uses string-length thresholds to restrict what paradigm models the Linguistica algorithm produces.

Excluding short types during ParaMor's morphology induction stage does not preclude short types from being analyzed as containing multiple morphemes during ParaMor's segmentation stage. As section 2.2 describes, ParaMor's segmentation algorithm is independent of the set of types from which schemes and scheme clusters are built.

The string length that types must meet to join the induction vocabulary is a free parameter. ParaMor is designed to identify the productive inflectional paradigms of a language. Unless a paradigm is restricted to occur only with short stems, a possible but unusual scenario (as with the English adjectival comparative, c.f. *faster* but **exquisiter*) we can expect a productive paradigm to occur with a reasonable number of longer stems in a corpus. Hence, ParaMor needn't be overly concerned about discarding short types. A qualitative examination of Spanish data suggested discarding types five characters or less in length; we use this cutoff in all experiments described in this paper.

Excluding short types from the paradigm induction vocabulary virtually eliminates the entire category of chance scheme. In a random sample of 100 schemes that ParaMor selected when short types were excluded, only one scheme contained types related only by chance string similarity, down from 35 when short types were not excluded. Returning to Table 1, excluding types five characters or less in length bars ten of the twelve word types which support the erroneous 3000th selected scheme *Ø.a.-anar*. Among the excluded types are valid Spanish words such as *ganar 'to gain'*. But also eliminated are several meaningless acronyms such as the single letters *g* and *s*. Without these short types, ParaMor rightly cannot select the 3000th scheme.

## 2.2 Segmentation

#### An Agglutinative Model

With the improvement in scheme precision that results from the two extensions discussed in section 2.1, we are ready to propose a more realistic model of morphology. ParaMor's baseline segmentation algorithm distrusts ParaMor's induced scheme models. The baseline algorithm assumes each word form can contain at most a single morpheme boundary. If it detects more than one morpheme boundary, then the baseline algorithm proposes a separate morphological analysis for each possible boundary. In contrast, our extended model of segmentation vests more trust in the induced schemes, assuming that scheme clusters which propose different morpheme boundaries are simply modeling different valid morpheme boundaries. And our extension proposes a single morphological analysis containing all hypothesized morpheme boundaries.

To detect morpheme boundaries, ParaMor matches each word, *w*, in the full vocabulary of a corpus against the clusters of schemes which are the final output of ParaMor's paradigm identification stage. When a suffix, *f*, of some scheme-cluster, *C*, matches a word-final string of *w*, i.e. $w = u.f$, ParaMor attempts to replace *f* in turn with each suffix $f'$ of *C*. If the string $u.f'$ occurs in the full corpus vocabulary, then, on the basis of this paradigmatic evidence, ParaMor identifies a morpheme boundary in *w* between *u* and *f*.

For example, to detect morpheme boundaries in the Spanish word *apoyados* 'supports *(adjective masculine plural)*', ParaMor matches all word-final strings of *apoyados* against the candidate suffixes of ParaMor's induced scheme clusters. The word-final strings of *apoyados* are *s*, *os*, *dos*, *ados*, *yados*, .... The scheme clusters that our extended version of ParaMor induces include clusters which contain schemes very similar to the 1st, 2nd, and 5th baseline selected schemes, see Table 1. In particular, our extended ParaMor identifies separate scheme clusters that contain the candidate suffixes: *s* and *Ø*; *os* and *o*; and *ados* and *ado*. Substituting *Ø* for *s*, *o* for *os*, or *ado* for *ados* yields the Spanish string *apoyado* 'supports *(adjective masculine singular)*'. It so happens, that *apoyado* does occur in our Spanish corpus, and so ParaMor has found paradigmatic evidence for three morpheme boundaries. Crucially, our ParaMor extension from section 2.1 that removes schemes which hypothesize suffix internal morpheme boundaries correctly discards all schemes which contained the candidate suffix *dos*. Consequently, no scheme cluster exists to incorrectly suggest the morpheme boundary **apoya* + *dos*, as the 3rd baseline selected scheme would have. Where ParaMor's baseline segmentation algorithm would propose three separate analyses of *apoyados*, one for each detected morpheme boundary: *apoy +ados*, *apoyad +os*, and *apoyado +s*; our extended segmentation algorithm produces the single correct analysis: *apoy +ad +o +s*.

It is interesting to note that although each of ParaMor's individual paradigm models proposes a single morpheme boundary, our agglutinative segmentation model can recover multiple boundaries in a single word. Using this idea it may be possible to quickly adapt Linguistica for agglutinative languages. Instead of interpreting the sets of stems and affixes that Goldsmith's Linguistica algorithm produces as immediate segmentations of words, these signatures can be thought of as models of paradigms that may generalize to new words.

**Augmenting ParaMor's Segmentations**

With its focus on the paradigm, ParaMor specializes at analyzing inflectional morphology (Monson et al., 2007a). Morpho Challenge 2007 requires algorithms to analyze both inflectional and derivational morphology (Kurimo et al., 2007a; 2007b). To compete in the challenge, we combine ParaMor's morphological segmentations with segmentations from Morfessor (Creutz, 2006), an unsupervised morphology induction algorithm which learns both inflectional and derivational morphology. We incorporate the segmentations from Morfessor into the segmentations that the ParaMor system produces by straightforwardly adding the Morfessor segmentation for each word as an additional separate analysis to those ParaMor produces (Monson et al., 2007b). Morfessor has one free parameter, which we optimize separately for each language of Morpho Challenge 2007.

ParaMor also has several free parameters, including the type length parameter and the parameter over stem-final character entropy described in section 2.1. We do not adjust any of ParaMor's parameters from language to language, but fix them at values that produce reasonable Spanish paradigms and segmentations. As in Monson et al. (2007b), to avoid adjusting ParaMor's parameters we limit ParaMor's paradigm induction vocabulary to 50,000 frequent types for each language.

## 3 Evaluation

To evaluate our extensions to the ParaMor algorithm, we follow the methodology of the peer operated Morpho Challenge 2007. All segmentations produced by our extensions were sent to the Morpho Challenge Organizing Committee (Kurimo et al., 2008). The Organizing Committee evaluated our segmentations and returned the automatically calculated quantitative results. Using the evaluation methodology of Morpho Challenge 2007 permits us to compare our algorithms against the unsupervised morphology induction systems which competed in the 2007 Challenge. Of the many algorithms for unsupervised morphology induction discussed with the related work in section 1.1, five participated in Morpho Challenge 2007. Unless an algorithm has been given an explicit name, morphology induction algorithms will be denoted in this paper by the name of their lead author. The five algorithms which participated in the 2007 Challenge are: Bernhard (2007), Bordag (2007), Zeman (2007), Creutz's (2006) Morfessor, and ParaMor (2007b).

Morpho Challenge 2007 had participating algorithms analyze words in four languages: English, German, Finnish, and Turkish. The Challenge evaluated each algorithm's morphological analyses in two ways. First, a linguistic evaluation measured each algorithm's precision, recall, and $F_1$ at morpheme identification against an answer key of morphologically analyzed word forms. Scores were normalized when a system proposed multiple analyses of a single word, as our combined ParaMor-Morfessor submissions do. For further details on the linguistic evaluation in Morpho Challenge 2007, see Kurimo et al. (2007a). The second evaluation of Morpho Challenge 2007 was a task based evaluation. Each algorithm's analyses were imbedded in an information retrieval (IR) system. The IR evaluation consisted of queries over a language specific collection of newswire articles. All word forms in all queries and all documents were replaced with the morphological decompositions of each individual analysis algorithm. Separate IR tasks were run for English, German, and Finnish, but not Turkish. For additional details on the IR evaluation of Morpho Challenge 2007 please reference Kurimo et al. (2007b).

Tables 2 and 3 present, respectively, the linguistic and IR evaluation results. In these two tables, the top two rows contain results for segmentations produced by versions of ParaMor that include our extensions. The topmost row in each table, labeled '+P +Seg', gives the results for our fully augmented version of ParaMor, which includes our two extensions designed to improve precision as well as our new segmentation model which can propose multiple morpheme boundaries in a single analysis of a word form. The second row of each table, labeled '+P –Seg', augments ParaMor only with the two enhancements designed to improve precision. The third row of each table gives the Challenge results for the ParaMor baseline algorithm. Rows four through seven of each table give scores from Morpho Challenge 2007 for the best performing unsupervised systems. If multiple versions of a single algorithm competed in the Challenge, the scores reported here are the highest $F_1$ or Average Precision score of any algorithm variant at a particular task. In all test scenarios but Finnish IR, we produced Morfessor segmentations to augment ParaMor that are independent of the Morfessor runs which competed in Morpho Challenge. If our Morfessor runs gave a higher $F_1$ or Average Precision, then we report this higher score. Finally, scores reported on rows eight and beyond are from reference algorithms that are not unsupervised. Reference algorithms appear in *italics*. A double line bisects both Table 2 and Table 3 horizontally. All results which appear above the double line were evaluated after the final deadline of Morpho Challenge 2007. In particular, ParaMor officially competed only in the English and German tracks of the Challenge.

**The Linguistic Evaluation**

Table 2 contains the results from the linguistic evaluation of Morpho Challenge. The Morpho Challenge Organizing Committee did not provide us with data on the statistical significance of the results for the enhanced versions of ParaMor. But most score differences are statistically significant—All $F_1$ differences of more than 0.5 between systems which officially competed in Morpho Challenge 2007 were statistically significant (Kurimo et al., 2007a).

In German, Finnish, and Turkish our fully enhanced version of ParaMor achieves a higher $F_1$ than any system that competed in Morpho Challenge 2007. In English, ParaMor's precision score drags $F_1$ under that of the first place system, Bernhard; In Finnish, the Bernhard system's $F_1$ is likely not statistically different from that of our system. Our final segmentation algorithm demonstrates consistent performance across all four languages. In Turkish, where the morpheme recall of other unsupervised systems is anomalously low, our algorithm achieves a recall in a range similar to its recall scores for the other languages. ParaMor's ultimate recall is double that of any other unsuper-

| | | English | | | German | | | Finnish | | | Turkish | | |
|---|---|---|---|---|---|---|---|---|---|---|---|---|---|
| | | P | R | $F_1$ | P | R | $F_1$ | P | R | $F_1$ | P | R | $F_1$ |
| ParaMor & Morfessor | +P +Seg | 50.6 | 63.3 | 56.3 | 49.5 | **59.5** | 54.1 | 49.8 | **47.3** | **48.5** | 51.9 | **52.1** | **52.0** |
| | +P –Seg | 56.2 | 60.9 | 58.5 | 57.4 | 53.5 | **55.4** | 60.5 | 33.9 | 43.5 | 62.0 | 38.2 | 47.3 |
| | Baseline | 41.6 | **65.1** | 50.7 | 51.5 | 55.6 | 53.4 | 55.0 | 35.6 | 43.2 | 53.2 | 41.6 | 46.7 |
| Bernhard | | 61.6 | 60.0 | **60.8** | 49.1 | 57.4 | 52.9 | 59.7 | 40.4 | **48.2** | 73.7 | 14.8 | 24.7 |
| Bordag | | 59.7 | 32.1 | 41.8 | 60.5 | 41.6 | 49.3 | 71.3 | 24.4 | 36.4 | 81.3 | 17.6 | 28.9 |
| Morfessor | | 82.2 | 33.1 | 47.2 | 67.6 | 36.9 | 47.8 | 76.8 | 27.5 | 40.6 | 73.9 | 26.1 | 38.5 |
| Zeman | | 53.0 | 42.1 | 46.9 | 52.8 | 28.5 | 37.0 | 58.8 | 20.9 | 30.9 | 65.8 | 18.8 | 29.2 |
| *Tepper* | | *69.2* | *52.6* | *59.8* | - | - | - | *62.0* | *46.2* | *53.0* | *70.3* | *43.0* | *53.3* |

Table 2. Unsupervised morphology induction systems evaluated for precision (P), recall (R), and $F_1$ at morpheme identification using the methodology of the linguistic competition of Morpho Challenge 2007.

vised Turkish system, leading to an improvement in $F_1$ over the next best system, Morfessor alone, of 13.5% absolute or 22.0% relative.

In all four languages, as expected, the combination of removing short types from the training data, and the additional filtering of scheme clusters, '+P', significantly improves precision scores over the ParaMor baseline. Allowing multiple morpheme boundaries in a single word, '+Seg', increases the number of words ParaMor believes share a morpheme. Some of these new words do in fact share a morpheme, some, in reality do not. Hence, our extension of ParaMor to agglutinative sequences of morphemes increases recall but lowers precision across all four languages. The effect of agglutinative segmentations on $F_1$, however, differs with language. For the two languages which make limited use of suffix sequences, English and German, a model which hypothesizes multiple morpheme boundaries can only moderately increase recall and does not justify, by $F_1$, the many incorrect segmentations which result. On the other hand, an agglutinative model significantly improves recall for true agglutinative languages like Finnish and Turkish, more than compensating in $F_1$ for the drop in precision over these languages. But in all four languages, the agglutinative version of ParaMor outperforms the baseline unenhanced version at $F_1$.

The final row of Table 2 is the evaluation of a reference algorithm submitted by Tepper (2007). While not an unsupervised algorithm, Tepper's reference parallels ParaMor in augmenting segmentations produced by Morfessor. Where ParaMor augments Morfessor with special attention to inflectional morphology, Tepper augments Morfessor with hand crafted morphophonology rules that conflate multiple surface forms of the same underlying suffix. Like ParaMor, Tepper's algorithm significantly improves on Morfessor's recall. With two examples of successful system augmentation, we suggest that future research take a closer look at building on existing unsupervised morphology induction systems.

### The IR Evaluation

Turn now to results from the IR evaluation in Table 3. Although ParaMor does not fair as well in Finnish, in German, the fully enhanced version of ParaMor places above the best system from the 2007 Challenge, Bernhard, while our score on English rivals this same best system. Morpho Challenge 2007 did not measure the statistical significance of uninterpolated average precision scores in the IR evaluation. It is not clear what feature of ParaMor's Finnish analyses causes comparatively low average precision. Perhaps it is simply that ParaMor attains a lower morpheme recall over Finnish than over English or German. And unfortunately, Morpho Challenge 2007 did not run IR experiments over the other agglutinative language in the competition, Turkish. When ParaMor does not combine multiple morpheme boundaries into a single analysis, as in the baseline and '+P –Seg' sce-

| | | Eng. | Ger. | Finn. | Tur. |
|---|---|---|---|---|---|
| ParaMor & Morfessor | +P +Seg | 39.3 | **48.4** | 42.6 | - |
| | +P –Seg | 35.1 | 43.1 | 37.1 | - |
| | Baseline | 34.4 | 40.1 | 35.9 | - |
| **Bernhard** | | **39.4** | 47.3 | **49.2** | - |
| **Bordag** | | 34.0 | 43.1 | 43.1 | - |
| **Morfessor** | | 38.8 | 46.0 | 44.1 | - |
| **Zeman** | | 26.7* | 25.7* | 28.1* | - |
| ***Dummy*** | | *31.2* | *32.3* | *32.7* | - |
| ***Oracle*** | | *37.7* | *34.7* | *43.1* | - |
| ***Porter*** | | *40.8* | - | - | - |
| ***Tepper*** | | *37.3** | - | - | - |

Table 3. Unsupervised morphology induction systems evaluated for uninterpolated average precision using the methodology of the IR competition of Morpho Challenge 2007. These results use Okapi term weighting (Kurimo et al., 2008b).

*Only a subset of the words which occurred in the IR evaluation of this language was analyzed by this system.

narios, average precision is comparatively poor. Where the linguistic evaluation did not always penalize a system for proposing multiple partial analyses, real NLP applications, such as IR, can.

The reference algorithms for the IR evaluation are: Dummy, no morphological analysis; Oracle, where all words in the queries and documents for which the linguistic answer key contains an entry are replaced with that answer; Porter, the standard English Porter stemmer; and Tepper described above. While the hand built Porter stemmer still outperforms the best unsupervised systems on English, these same best unsupervised systems outperform both the Dummy and Oracle references for all three evaluated languages—strong evidence that unsupervised induction algorithms are not only better than no morphological analysis, but that they are better than incomplete analysis as well.

## 4 Conclusions and Future Directions

Augmenting ParaMor with an agglutinative model of segmentation produces an unsupervised morphology induction system with consistent and strong performance at morpheme identification across all four languages of Morpho Challenge 2007. By first cleaning up the paradigm models that ParaMor learns, we raise ParaMor's segmentation precision and allow the agglutinative model to significantly improve ParaMor's morpheme recall.

Looking forward to future improvements, we examined by hand the final set of scheme clusters that the current version of ParaMor produces over our newswire corpus of 50,000 Spanish types. ParaMor's paradigm identification stage outputs 41 separate clusters. Among these final scheme clusters are those which model all major productive paradigms of Spanish. In fact, there are often multiple scheme clusters which model portions of the same true paradigm. As an extreme case, 12 separate scheme clusters contain suffixes from the Spanish *ar* verbal paradigm. Relaxing restrictions on ParaMor's clustering algorithm (Monson et al., 2007a) may address this paradigm fragmentation.

The second significant shortcoming which surfaces among ParaMor's 41 final scheme clusters is that ParaMor currently does not address morphophonology. Among the final scheme clusters, 12 attempt to model morphophonological change by incorporating the phonological change either into the stems or into the suffixes of the scheme cluster. But ParaMor currently has no mechanism for detecting when a cluster is modeling morphophonology. Perhaps ideas on morphophonology from Goldsmith (2006) could be adapted to work with the ParaMor algorithm. Finally, we plan to look at scaling the size of the vocabulary used both during paradigm induction and during morpheme segmentation. We are particularly interested in the possibility that ParaMor may be able to identify paradigms from much less data than 50,000 types.

## Acknowledgements

We kindly thank Mikko Kurimo, Ville Turunen, Matti Varjokallio, and the full Organizing Committee of Morpho Challenge 2007, for running the evaluations of ParaMor. These dedicated workers produced impressively fast turn around for evaluations on sometimes rather short notice.

The research described in this paper was supported by NSF grants IIS-0121631 (AVENUE) and IIS-0534217 (LETRAS), with supplemental funding from NSF's Office of Polar Programs and Office of International Science and Education.

## References


Bernhard, Delphine. Simple Morpheme Labeling in Unsupervised Morpheme Analysis. *Working Notes for the CLEF 2007 Workshop*. Budapest, Hungary, 2007.

Bordag, Stefan. Unsupervised and Knowledge-free Morpheme Segmentation and Analysis. *Working Notes for the CLEF 2007 Workshop*. Budapest, Hungary, 2007.

Brent, Michael R., Sreerama K. Murthy, and Andrew Lundberg. Discovering Morphemic Suffixes: A Case Study in MDL Induction. *The Fifth International Workshop on Artificial Intelligence and Statistics*. Fort Lauderdale, Florida, 1995.

Creutz, Mathias. *Induction of the Morphology of Natural Language: Unsupervised Morpheme Segmentation with Application to Automatic Speech Recognition*. Ph.D. Thesis. Computer and Information Science, Report D13. Helsinki: University of Technology, Espoo, Finland, 2006.

Demberg, Vera, Helmut Schmid, and Gregor Möhler. Phonological Constraints and Morphological Preprocessing for Grapheme-to-Phoneme Conversion. *Association for Computational Linguistics*. Prague, Czech Republic, 2007.

Dryer, Matthew S. Prefixing vs. Suffixing in Inflectional Morphology. In *The World Atlas of Language Structures*. Eds. Martin Haspelmath, Matthew S. Dryer, David Gil, and Bernard Comrie. 2005.

Goldsmith, John. Unsupervised Learning of the Morphology of a Natural Language. *Computational Linguistics*. 27.2:153-198. 2001.

Goldsmith, John. An Algorithm for the Unsupervised Learning of Morphology. *Natural Language Engineering*. 12.4:335-351. 2006.

Goldsmith, John, and Yu Hu. From Signatures to Finite State Automata. Paper presented at the Midwest Computational Linguistics Colloquium. Bloomington, Indiana, 2004.

Goldwater, Sharon, and David McClosky. Improving Statistic MT through Morphological Analysis. *Empirical Methods in Natural Language Processing*. Vancouver, Canada, 2005.

Hafer, Margaret A. and Stephen F. Weiss. Word Segmentation by Letter Successor Varieties. *Information Storage and Retrieval*, 10:371-385. 1974.

Harris, Zellig. From Phoneme to Morpheme. *Language* 31.2:190-222. 1955. Reprinted in Harris (1970).

Harris, Zellig. *Papers in Structural and Transformational Linguists*. Ed. D. Reidel, Dordrecht. 1970.

Johnson, Howard, and Joel Martin. Unsupervised Learning of Morphology for English and Inuktitut. *Human Language Technology Conference / North American Chapter of the Association for Computational Linguistics*. Edmonton, Canada, 2003.

Kurimo, Mikko, Mathias Creutz, and Matti Varjokallio. Unsupervised Morpheme Analysis Evaluation by a Comparison to a Linguistic Gold Standard – Morpho Challenge 2007. *Working Notes for the CLEF 2007 Workshop*. Budapest, Hungary, 2007a.

Kurimo, Mikko, Mathias Creutz, and Ville Turunen. Unsupervised Morpheme Analysis Evaluation by IR Experiments – Morpho Challenge 2007. *Working Notes for the CLEF 2007 Workshop*. Budapest, Hungary, 2007b.

Kurimo, Mikko, Mathias Creutz, and Matti Varjokallio. Unsupervised Morpheme Analysis -- Morpho Challenge 2007. January 10, 2008. <http://www.cis.hut.-fi/morphochallenge2007/>. 2008.

Monson, Christian, Jaime Carbonell, Alon Lavie, and Lori Levin. ParaMor: Minimally Supervised Induction of Paradigm Structure and Morphological Analysis. *Computing and Historical Phonology: The Ninth Meeting of the ACL Special Interest Group in Computational Morphology and Phonology*. Prague, Czech Republic, 2007a.

Monson, Christian, Jaime Carbonell, Alon Lavie, and Lori Levin. ParaMor: Finding Paradigms across Morphology. *Working Notes for the CLEF 2007 Workshop*. Budapest, Hungary, 2007b.

Schone, Patrick, and Daniel Jurafsky. Knowledge-Free Induction of Inflectional Morphologies. *North American Chapter of the Association for Computational Linguistics*. Pittsburgh, Pennsylvania, 2001.

Snover, Matthew G. *An Unsupervised Knowledge Free Algorithm for the Learning of Morphology in Natural Languages*. M.S. Thesis. Computer Science, Sever Institute of Technology, Washington University, Saint Louis, Missouri, 2002.

Tepper, Michael A. Using Hand-Written Rewrite Rules to Induce Underlying Morphology. *Working Notes for the CLEF 2007 Workshop*. Budapest, Hungary, 2007.

Wicentowski, Richard. *Modeling and Learning Multilingual Inflectional Morphology in a Minimally Supervised Framework*. Ph.D. Thesis. Johns Hopkins University, Baltimore, Maryland, 2002.

Zeman, Daniel. Unsupervised Acquiring of Morphological Paradigms from Tokenized Text. *Working Notes for the CLEF 2007 Workshop*. Budapest, Hungary, 2007.

**Association for Computational Linguistics**
209 N. Eighth Street
Stroudsburg, Pennsylvania 18360